13

A Historical Surv

13 MAY 1969
A HISTORICAL SURVEY OF SINO-MALAY RELATIONS

LEON COMBER

Graham Brash (Pte) Ltd
36-C Prinsep Street
Singapore 0718

First published in 1983.
This edition first published in 1988
by Graham Brash (Pte) Ltd
36-C Prinsep Street
Singapore 0718

ISBN 9971-49-085-4

Cover illustration by Teo Kim Heng
Printed by Chong Moh Offset Printing Pte Ltd, Singapore

To the 'Children of 13 May'

Contents

List of Plates

Between pages 50 and 51

Foreword

It gives me great pleasure to pen a few words of introduction for Leon Comber's historical survey of Sino-Malay relations, leading up to the 13 May 1969 disturbances.

Mr. Comber is indeed well qualified to write this account as he has a good working knowledge of our national language, Bahasa Malaysia, as well as being well versed in Chinese, and as a Malaysian citizen, he is one of the select band of Europeans who has a deep and warm appreciation of our culture and way of life.

It is the only work I know which attempts to provide in such a clear, concise and objective form the main scenario of Sino-Malay relations in Malaysia for the layman to follow. Mr. Comber's style is lucid and attractive, which makes his book easy to read, and he deals with quite complicated issues in a refreshingly clear way. I feel sure that future scholars will be greatly indebted to Mr. Comber's work for providing the framework on which further detailed research may be carried out.

I wish Mr. Comber's book all the success which it deserves and I hope that many of our people will read and benefit from it.

(Tunku Abdul Rahman Putra)

Author's Preface

On 15 March 1981, the *New Straits Times* published the following letter from Maarof Bakar, who described himself as a labourer:

'Many young people, now in their twenties, were eyewitnesses to the race riots of May 13, 1969. They will never be able to forget what they saw.

'They were children then, aged between 10 and 15. But they were old enough to understand what was happening, young enough to be observers rather than participants.

'The images of buildings on fire, soldiers carrying guns through the streets, racial violence, racial hatred and prejudices were magnified in their eyes.

'Today, they are young adults. They feel they have an important mission. They feel they have a responsibility to always remind themselves and others of the time they saw the power of destruction that can be unleashed when emotion defeats reason.

'They search for answers to the questions that disturb them. They search the past, the history of this nation. No group of people are so intense about finding reasons for the riots they witnessed as children. No group of people in this land show greater interest towards race-relations as they do.

'I call them the children of 13 May, and I am proud to be one of them.'

This study, then, is dedicated to the 'children of 13 May' in the hope that it will help them to understand the questions which still haunt them. It is based on an acquaintance (and fascination) with Malaysia extending over thirty-five years, when the author who was then a young staff officer on 34th Indian Corps headquarters, first landed on the west coast of Malaya near Port Swettenham in September 1945 with the 'Operation Zipper' invasion force. However, the actual research and writing was spread over two years or so, and was originally presented as a dissertation in part fulfilment of the degree of MA in Comparative Asian Studies at the University of Hong Kong.

I am particularly indebted to Dr. Mary Turnbull, Professor Peter Harris, Dr. Leigh Wright, Professor Khoo Kay Kim, Professor Syed Hussein Alatas, Dr. Chandra Muzaffar, Dennis Bloodworth and Leonard Rayner for help in various ways.

I would also like to record my indebtedness to Rupert Emerson's classic study, *Malaysia, A Study in Direct and Indirect Rule,* and other works listed in the Bibliography, without which this book could not have been written.

Acknowledgements

Thanks are due to the following authors and publishers for permission to reproduce copyright material from the works indicated: Ooi Jin-Bee and Longman Group Ltd., *Peninsula Malaysia;* R.K. Vasil and Oxford University Press, *The Malaysian General Elections of 1969;* Rupert Emerson and The University of Malaya Press, *Malaysia, A Study in Direct and Indirect Rule; New Straits Times* of 15 March 1981; Government Printer, Singapore, *The Economic Development of Malaya: Report of a Mission organised by the International Bank for Reconstruction and Development;* and Government Press, Kuala Lumpur, *Mid-Term Review of the Second Malaysia Plan 1971—1975*.

Abbreviations

AMCJA	All-Malaya Council of Joint Action
CIA	Central Intelligence Agency
CLC	Communities Liaison Committee
DAP	Democratic Action Party
FAMA	Federal Agricultural Marketing Authority
FELDA	Federal Land Development Authority
FMS	Federated Malay States
IMP	Independence of Malaya Party
KMM	Kesatuan Melayu Muda (Association of Malay Youths)
KMT	Kuomintang (Chinese Nationalist Party)
KRIS	Kesatuan Ra'ayat Indonesia Semenanjong (People's Association of the Indonesian Peninsula)
LPM	Labour Party of Malaya
MARA	Majlis Amanah Ra'ayat (Council of Trust for the Indigenous People)
MAS	Malay Administrative Service
MCA	Malayan/Malaysian Chinese Association
MCP	Malayan Communist Party
MIC	Malayan/Malaysian Indian Congress
MCS	Malayan Civil Service
MNP	Malay Nationalist Party
MPABA	Malayan People's Anti-British Army
MPAJA	Malayan People's Anti-Japanese Army
MPAJU	Malayan People's Anti-Japanese Union
MRLA	Malayan Races Liberation Army
NCC	National Consultative Council
NEP	New Economic Policy
NOC	National Operations Council
PAP	People's Action Party
PERNAS	Perbadanan Nasional Berhad (State Trading Corporation)
PETA	Pembela Tanah Ayer (Defenders of the Motherland)
PMIP	Pan Malaysian Islamic Party
PPP	People's Progressive Party
RIDA	Rural and Industrial Development Authority
SMP	Second Malaysia Plan 1971-75
SEDC	State Economic Development Corporation
UDA	Urban Development Authority
UDP	United Democratic Party
UMNO	United Malays National Organization
UMS	Unfederated Malay States

Introduction

This small volume is an attempt to chronicle the long road to the 13 May 1969 riots in Kuala Lumpur, which were acknowledged by the Malaysian authorities to be the most serious racial riots in the history of the country. It is not primarily concerned with recounting the events of that tragic occasion, but is an attempt to lay bare the underlying reasons for what happened and to provide a comprehensive, yet concise, historical picture of the complex Sino-Malay relationship in Peninsular Malaysia, for both layman and student of race relations alike.

In order to do this, the interplay of the two main communities in Peninsular Malaysia, the Malays and Chinese, has been scrutinized from a historical viewpoint, going back to the time of the earliest Chinese settlements in Malaya.

It was only after the tremendous influx of Chinese immigrants in the second half of the nineteenth century that Sino-Malay friction began to grow. There were differences of customs, language, food and religion. But, more importantly, the 'world view' of the two communities was poles apart too. The Chinese were xenophobic and sinocentric. On the other hand, the social and religious structure of the Malays made it impossible for any other religious or ethnic group, with the exception of Arabs or Indian-Muslims, to be integrated with them. Intermarriage between the two communities, which would have helped to break down racial barriers, was extremely rare, as the non-Malay partner would be required to embrace the Muslim faith.

Most of the early Chinese immigrants were in the true sense of the word 'aliens', and moreover, transient aliens, as the great majority of them had no intention of settling in Malaya but only of seeking their fortune and, if they were fortunate enough, returning, wealthier than they had ever dreamed of, to their ancestral villages in China. However, as the twentieth century progressed there was a growing number of local-born Chinese who began to think of Malaya as their home and who had no intention of returning to China. It was this section of the Chinese community which began to demand citizenship rights and some say in the running of the country.

When the 1931 Census revealed for the first time that the Malays were outnumbered in their own country by the non-Malays, it came as something of a shock to both the Malays and the British colonial authorities. The Malays were concerned about preserving their heritage and birthright as the indigenous people of the country, a factor which had been recognized by the British in the treaties entered into with the Malay rulers much earlier on. Restrictions were imposed on further immigration by Chinese, and steps were taken to control Chinese schools, which were 'alien enclaves' teaching Chinese values and loyalties inappropriate to the Malayan setting.

The Japanese occupation (1942–5) gave the British Colonial Office time to 'rethink' the situation and to formulate plans for the reoccupation of the country after the Japanese had been defeated. In the meantime, Japanese rule exacerbated the ill-feeling between the Malay and Chinese communities. Although both communities suffered, the Chinese were the worse off because they were distrusted by the Japanese, especially as China had been at war with Japan since 1937, and Chinese communist and other volunteer units had put up a stiff resistance to the Japanese during the closing stages of the battle for Singapore.

The Malayan Union plan which the British introduced on their return to Malaya in 1945 did not find favour in Malay eyes, as it gave away too much to the non-Malays, and it had to be withdrawn and replaced by the Federation of Malaya Agreement, which reaffirmed the 'special position' of the Malays and recognized the sultans as sovereign monarchs, which meant *ipso facto* that the Federation of Malaya was a Malay state.

By the early 1950s, it was clear that the main grounds for dissatisfaction and resentment on the part of the Chinese were their lack of citizenship rights; the national language issue, which they feared would lead to the stamping out of the Chinese language and culture; the national education policy, favouring Malay as the medium of instruction; and what they perceived as the privileged 'special position' of the Malays.

In order to present a united front to the Reid Constitutional Commission which was drafting the constitution for an independent Malaya, UMNO and the MCA leaders agreed in 1956 to a 'bargain' or 'pact' whereby the MCA conceded Malay 'special rights' in return for more liberal citizenship terms, as well as a free hand for the Chinese in pursuing their economic and commercial interests.

As Tunku Abdul Rahman put it in 1969, 'The Malays have gained for themselves political power. The Chinese and Indians have won for themselves economic power' (see p. 64). It is indeed, this 'bargain' which has bedevilled Sino-Malay relations in more recent times, as the younger generation of Chinese do not wish to abide by it. Moreover, the matter was not made any better by the People's Action Party's campaigning in the 1964 Malaysian general elections for a 'Malaysian Malaysia', and Prime Minister Lee Kuan Yew's challenging the 'special rights' of the Malays, which was to lead to Singapore's expulsion from Malaysia. In fact, the electioneering leading up to the 1969 federal and state elections released dangerous pent-up racial feelings and emotions both on the Malay and the Chinese sides, and it seemed as if both communities were moving inexorably towards a massive confrontation on a scale which had never before been envisaged.

The spilling of blood on 13 May 1969, and the terrible disturbances which followed, almost tore the country asunder. Parliament was suspended for twenty months and the country was ruled by a National Operations Council. By the time parliament resumed, many changes had taken place. Tunku Abdul Rahman was no longer prime minister. He had resigned in September 1970 after leading the country as a multiracial symbol for fifteen years. The *Rukunegara,* or official state ideology, had been announced, and a 'New Economic Policy' (NEP) had been unwrapped. Several contentious and potentially dangerous matters dealing, for example, with Malay 'special rights', the national language, religion, and so on, had been removed from the domain of discussion not only in public but also in the hitherto privileged confines of the Dewan Rakyat and the state legislatures. The *Rukunegara* made it evident that neither the Malay nor Chinese extremists were going to be able to claim victory, as it tried to steer a middle path between the interests of the two communities.

The New Economic Policy, which has been spelt out in detail in the *Second Malaysia Plan 1971—1975*, follows a two-pronged approach: the restructuring of the economy to 'correct economic imbalance' between the Malays and the Chinese, and the eradication of poverty among all Malaysians.

If the spirit of the NEP is adhered to in practice, so that, as the plan says, 'no particular group will experience any loss or feel any sense of deprivation', then there can be no objection to it, but obviously much depends on the way in which the policy is interpreted and administered by the Malaysian authorities.

The cut-off point of this account is the resumption of parliament in February 1971, as what happens after that marks the beginning of yet another panel in the unfolding scroll of Sino-Malay relations.

In dealing with the 13 May 1969 racial riots and Sino-Malay friction, attention has been focused on what happened in Peninsular Malaysia rather than in Singapore or Sabah and Sarawak, and events in the latter three territories have been referred to only when they have a bearing on the subject of this book.

Chapter One

The Beginnings of Plural Society in Malaya: Chinese and Malays

Since A.D. 414, when Fa Hsien, the intrepid Buddhist monk and pilgrim, stayed in Java for five months on his way back to China after a stay of fifteen years in India, the Chinese have continued to visit the *Nanyang* (Southeast Asia) in increasing numbers. However, as far as the Malay Peninsula is concerned, the earliest record that we have from Chinese sources of a Chinese colony there comes from the account of Wang Ta-yuan, who in 1349 mentions Tumasik, or old Singapore.[1]

The first significant Chinese settlements on the islands of the Malay archipelago date from as early as the thirteenth century. At San-fo-ts'i, in the neighbourhood of Palembang in Sumatra, there were several thousand Chinese, and it was one of the important ports of call for junks from China and ships from India.[2] Nevertheless, perhaps the best known early contacts with Malaya occurred during the early Ming dynasty, when the Chinese eunuch admiral Cheng Ho visited Malacca several times in the first half of the fifteenth century, and his name is still commemorated there in its deified form as Sam-po-kong.[3] One of his secretaries, Fei Sin, writing in 1436, reported that there were some people of Chinese descent living there,[4] which seems quite likely as it is customary to date the history of Chinese settlements in Malaya to after the establishment of the Malacca Sultanate *circa* 1400.[5]

Malacca was probably the first and certainly the largest place of any Chinese settlement in Peninsular Malaya, although there were other long-established communities of Chinese traders living usually in the Malay rulers' villages situated at the river mouth, where the Malay chiefs could control riverine trade and impose a tax on it. Some of these were permanently settled communities whose founders had married local women, and their offspring formed the nucleus of what later, during the nineteenth century, became known as the 'Straits Chinese' or *babas*.[6] The main centres of the *babas* were Malacca and Penang. They did not regard themselves as merely temporary immigrants in search of a living but as settlers. Many of them did not speak any Chinese at all but only Malay, although they adhered to a Chinese way of life which was influenced by Malay and other local customs.

Meanwhile, the network of Chinese traders grew. There were a thousand Chinese families from other places who settled in Johore in the early eighteenth century. It was estimated that in 1720 half the population of Kuala Trengganu was Chinese. The Chinese in Johore were mainly pepper cultivators and in Trengganu, traders. In the latter state they mined for gold too. The Trengganu Chinese owned junks and traded with Siam, Cambodia, Tongking and Sambas in Borneo.[7] In Perak, Chinese miners had worked tin since at least the eighteenth century, and they played an important role in the development of tin mining in Selangor in the 1780s.[8]

In the early decades of the nineteenth century, Chinese immigrants began to move into the western Peninsular Malay States following the discovery of tin deposits in Malacca (Linggi), Perak (Larut) and Selangor (Klang). The owners of the mines were Malay chiefs, but much of the finance was provided by Chinese and western entrepreneurs in the Straits Settlements, in particular from Singapore and Penang. Although the direct employers of Chinese labour were invariably Chinese lessees or contractors, the Chinese labourers were called in by the Malay chiefs.[9]

This was the beginning of a flood of Chinese immigration which was eventually to change the racial composition of the country. Before 1850, for instance, there were reported to be only three Chinese in Larut, but by 1862 there were 20,000 to 25,000 and by 1877 about 40,000.[10] At this time, it should be noted that there were only 150,000 Malays in the west coast states of Perak, Selangor, and Negri Sembilan.[11] In 1907, it was estimated that there were 229,778 Chinese engaged in tin-mining in the Federated Malay States of Selangor, Perak, Negri Sembilan and Pahang. By the beginning of the twentieth century, Chinese formed 65 per cent of the population of Selangor, that is, twice the Malay population, and 46 per cent of the population of Perak, where they were about equal in numbers to the Malays.[12]

The Chinese were also active in many other sectors of the economy. For instance, they cultivated spices, pepper and gambier in Penang, Province Wellesley and Singapore. Nutmegs and cloves, planted by Chinese, remained an important crop of Penang and Province Wellesley until around 1860, when the plantations were destroyed by disease.[13] When the pepper plantations cultivated by Chinese planters in Singapore became exhausted around 1840, the planters concerned moved into Johore. The cultivation of sugar cane was carried out by Chinese in Province Wellesley and Krian. Tapioca was yet another crop which was planted successfully by Chinese in the Malacca area until it was replaced by the more profitable rubber in the 1890s.

Chinese labourers were employed, too, in clearing the jungle, building roads, and more important, with their strong commercial instincts and knowledge of the use of money, they assumed the role of retailers and small shopkeepers.

Although virtually none of the Chinese who immigrated to Malaya brought with them wealth, some of them prospered and they eventually came to fill every rung of Malaya's economic and social life. In a sense, they formed a complete and separate economic community in Malaya, ranging from labourers to a large middle class of shopkeepers, merchants, tradesmen and entrepreneurs, at the apex of which was a smaller group of capitalists who had fought their way up to head business enterprises of immense complexity, such as banks, insurance companies, shipping companies, tin mines and rubber estates.[14]

With each successive wave of immigration of Chinese male labourers from south China — very few Chinese women came until the second decade of the twentieth century — there were some who decided to stay on and make Malaya their permanent home. However, their average length of stay in Malaya was not more than seven years[15] as most of them had the intention of saving a modest sum sufficient to purchase land in their ancestral village and of returning to China.

There were several factors which encouraged immigration from south China on an increased scale during the second part of the nineteenth century. There was great unrest in south China which was the centre of the disturbances caused by the Taiping Uprising (1850–64). Neither food nor employment opportunities were able to keep pace with the increase in population. To many Chinese, therefore, the Malay States were a 'new frontier' offering opportunities of economic advancement which were not available in China itself. There was the attraction, too, of being able to earn higher wages than could be earned in China (even though some authorities have compared the lot of the Chinese immigrants with 'serfs'), as well as a chance, if one were frugal enough, of saving money which could be remitted to relatives in China.[16] Additionally, compared with China itself and other parts of Southeast Asia at that time, there was at least an acceptable modicum of law and order in Malaya, and it was known that the British administration ensured the enforcement of private property rights.

In spite of their large numbers, or perhaps because of them, as they preferred to keep together wherever possible in large family and clan groups, the Chinese remained aloof from the Malay community and lived completely separated social and economic lives. There was the spatial element too. The Chinese tended to congregate in the urban settlements whereas the Malays traditionally lived in their *kampungs* (villages) around the lower reaches of the major rivers. In the large urban settlements, 'Chinatowns' grew up in the business centres and the Malays built their houses on the outskirts.[17] The Chinese, apart from the *baba* community, represented an alien element in Malaya. They spoke their own language, which hardly any non-Chinese spoke in Malaya at that time, and followed their own distinctive way of life and customs. They tended, therefore, to be segregated in their own sector of the towns, and in their own *kongsis* (labourers' lines) on tin mines and rubber estates.[18] This separation was, in fact, tacitly encouraged by the British, and in the old town plans prepared by British architects and engineers of that period provision was invariably made for a clearly demarcated sector of each town to be reserved as the Chinese quarter, as indeed similar areas were reserved for Indians, Arabs and Europeans.[19]

It should be noted that this segregation did not represent any divide-and-rule policy on the part of the British, as it antedated the British arrival, but it was endemic to the whole region and beyond, even before the days of the Malacca Ṣultanate. It was simply that the different racial groups preferred to live in their own areas, where they could feel at ease among their own people, and where they would not encounter problems on account of language, food, customs and religion. Administration was made simpler, too, by the practice of appointing a *capitan,* or headman, for each group, who was responsible to the authorities for the conduct of the persons under his supervision.

The racial composition of Peninsular Malaya from 1835 to

1970, which is indicated by percentages of the total population in Appendix 1, shows very clearly the phenomenal increase in the Chinese population from a low of 7.7 per cent as opposed to 85.9 per cent Malays in 1835, to 29.4 per cent as against 63.9 per cent Malays in 1884, until in 1970 the Chinese made up 35.4 per cent of the total population. However, if the other substantial non-Malay element of the population, that is, Indian, is added to the Chinese figures, the position of the Malays is made even more precarious, as demonstrated below:

PERCENTAGE OF POPULATION (Peninsular Malaya)

Racial Group	*1884*	*1921*	*1931*	*1947*	*1957*	*1965*	*1970*
Malays	63.9	54.0	49.2	49.5	49.8	50.1	53.2
Chinese and Indians combined	29.4	44.5	49.0	49.2	48.5	47.9	46.0

It should be noted that these figures exclude the Straits Settlements of Singapore, Penang and Malacca, and as these were predominantly Chinese settlements, it can be seen that by 1931 the Malays had become a minority in their own country.

In keeping with the xenophobic and sinocentric attitude adopted by Chinese towards all foreigners, who were traditionally regarded as 'outer barbarians' and 'foreign devils', the Chinese tended to look down on Malays, and criticize them for being lazy, backward and pleasure-loving.

On the other hand, the Malays, who are Muslims, were socially exclusive. For the Malay, the sense of community is inextricably bound up with the concept of a community of true believers. Malays have a strong feeling of racial identity which is reinforced by Muslim attitudes towards *kafirs* (unbelievers), and they, in turn, did not hold the Chinese in very high esteem and commonly referred to them as *orang berhala* (worshippers of idols), without a *kitab* (holy book), meaning in this context the Koran. This feeling was undoubtedly accentuated by the incompatibility with Islam of certain Chinese habits, such as the keeping of pigs and the eating of 'unclean meat' (pork), which is expressly forbidden to all followers of the Muslim faith.

From the evidence available, it would seem that an acceptable definition of a Malay around the mid-nineteenth century would be a person professing the Muslim religion, habitually speaking

Malay, conforming to Malay *adat* (custom), and owing allegiance to his Malay ruler. There was no sense of national loyalty, as this did not develop until the Second World War, but only a more parochial loyalty to the Malay ruler of the state concerned.

It is patent that there was no way in which the Chinese could fit into the above category. In any case, as has been said above, intermarriage between the two communities, which would have helped to break down racial barriers, was very rare, especially as the non-Malay partner would be required to accept the Muslim faith. Moreover, as one Malay put it rather pithily, for a Malay to marry a Chinese would be like 'eating curry without sambal', the latter ingredient being the highly flavoured and pungent condiment eaten with curry to make it tastier.[20] In fact, it may be said that the social and religious structure of the Malays made it impossible for any other religious or ethnic community, with the exception of Arabs or Indian-Muslims, to be integrated with them.[21]

In the middle of the nineteenth century, however, the Malays did not feel that their position had been unduly threatened by the great influx of Chinese immigrants, as the majority of the Chinese had no intention of settling permanently in Malaya. Nevertheless, by the twentieth century the position had changed, and there was an increasing awareness and anxiety about the growing numbers of local-born Chinese who, although they may not have been assimilable, were undoubtedly putting down roots in Malaya, and driving the Malays off the land.[22]

While there were Malays working as rubber tappers and tin miners, and in other sectors of the economy, they were not participating in the modernization and opening up of their country; this move was being spearheaded by western and Chinese interests, and it was evident that the Malays preferred to follow their own rhythm of life in the *kampungs,* where they could grow rice and coconuts, keep chickens, or in the coastal areas combine subsistence agriculture with fishing, and remain their own masters. Rice cultivation was seasonal, and the actual work occupied only about two months a year, although the yield was sufficient for the entire year. The rest of the year could therefore be spent at leisure, as the country was well endowed with natural resources and there was, generally speaking, no need for anyone to go hungry.

The Malays traditionally had a strong, almost mystical, attachment to the land, which was connected with their underlying animistic beliefs, similar to those of the Javanese for their *tanah air* (homeland).[23] For instance, to protect the soul-substance of his staple food of rice, the Malay farmer performed a series of ritual acts to propitiate the spirits and supernatural powers, and resorted to divination to ascertain the best time to begin agricultural activity. Indeed, practices of this nature pre-date Islam, and are often encountered in Malay traditional life not far below the surface of the more orthodox Islamic overlay.[24] They relate back to the time when animism was the indigenous belief of the Malays. Moreover, in this connection, the influence of Hinduism, which was brought to Malaya by Indian traders before the coming of Islam, should also not be overlooked.

A rationalization of the Malay perception of themselves would be that they regarded themselves as the subjects of their own hereditary *rajas* to whom they gave their allegiance and loyalty, rather in the same way that a feudal vassal owes fealty to his liege lord. They felt that their place was in their *kampungs,* looking after the land, which they regarded as their birthright and heritage, and not working as cash labourers for westerners or Chinese.

It is therefore inaccurate and unfair to describe the Malays as 'indolent' and 'lotus eaters', as many non-Malay observers have done.[25] The situation is not as starkly simple as all that and it may well be that Malay perceptions and values were different in regard to commercial and industrial aspects of life.

Chapter Two

The Special Position of the Malays: Historical Background

After the initial forward movement of the British in Malaya[1] which resulted in the acquisition of Penang in 1786, Singapore in 1819 and Malacca in 1824, it was not until the 1870s that further large-scale advances were made.

Although the British government was opposed to the idea of interfering in the internal affairs of the Malay states, the energetic Sir Andrew Clarke, who arrived as governor of the Straits Settlements in 1873, had nevertheless been instructed by the Secretary of State to look into the affairs of the Malay Peninsula 'to consider whether it would be advisable to appoint a British officer to reside in any of the States ....'[2]

Within a short time of his arrival, Clarke seemed to have decided that intervention was the best policy. The first point of penetration was the state of Perak, where serious fighting had been going on between rival secret society factions, to which the Chinese tin miners belonged, to gain control of the lucrative tin mines. Warring factions among the Malays were also drawn in. As the governor was quite convinced that the Malay chiefs were incapable of dealing with the situation, he invited them and the Chinese secret society leaders to attend a conference at Pangkor Island in 1874. The main purpose of this meeting was to ask the rival Chinese groups to accept British arbitration to bring the fighting to an end and to decide on the succession to the throne of Perak.

As a result of this conference, the Pangkor Engagement was drawn up, which served as a model for agreements covering further British expansion in the Malay Peninsula. The terms of this agreement provided for the accrediting of a British Resident to the sultan's court 'whose advice must be asked and acted upon on all questions other than those touching Malay religion and custom'[3] although the sultan's powers and functions in other respects were not meant to be curtailed.

Within a few months, Clarke had made similar agreements with Selangor and Sungei Ujong, a small state in Negri Sembilan just south of the Selangor border, by which both states agreed to accept British Residents.[4]

The Residential system first established in Perak, Selangor and the small state of Sungei Ujong, was later extended to Negri Sembilan and Pahang, and in 1896, these west coast states were joined together as the Federated Malay States (FMS).[5] This grouping has been described as neither a real federation nor a union but as being closer to a union in spirit, and the British Residents came under the supervision of a British Resident-General in Kuala Lumpur, who in turn was responsible to the Governor of the Straits Settlements in Singapore wearing his other hat as High Commissioner of the FMS.[6] The more important government departments in each state reported back to federal departmental heads in the federal capital of Kuala Lumpur. In other words, the British hold on the administration of the states was tightened, although the interests of the Malay rulers were respected and, at least ostensibly, decisions continued to be made in their names.

At this point it might be useful to cite an opinion regarding the position of the Malay sultans which was given by Resident-General Sir William Treacher in 1903. 'Long before the date of federalization' he wrote, 'the Sultan had ceased to ask and take the advice of the Resident on all questions other than those touching Mahomedan *(sic)* religion and Malay custom, but that on the contrary it has become the practice for the Resident with the sanction of the Governor of the Straits Settlements (now the High Commissioner of the Federated Malay States) to frame annual estimates of revenue and expenditure, to make official appointments and to do a hundred and one other things, not touching Mahomedan *(sic)* religion or Malay custom, without reference to the Sultan; and this is a correct statement. The position has in fact been reversed: instead of the Sultan carrying on the Government with the advice of the Resident (Mahomedan *(sic)* religion and custom excepted), the Resident carried on the administration with the reference when he considers it necessary for the advice of the Sultan. Whether that is right or wrong I need not now inquire, but it is an incontestable fact'.[7]

Not long afterwards, the five remaining states of Kedah, Perlis, Kelantan, Trengganu and Johore were induced to accept British Advisers (not 'Residents', so as to emphasize, as it were, that they were what the title implied and not 'executive officers'), and these states became known as the Unfederated Malay States (UMS). Their Malay rulers tended to retain more independence than their counterparts in the FMS, and their relations with Britain were carried on by direct contact with the Governor in Singapore, and not through the Resident-General in Kuala Lumpur. They had no special inner ties among themselves but the UMS, the FMS, and the Straits Settlements of Penang, Singapore and Malacca made up what was known as British Malaya.[8]

The British administrators in Malaya generally tended to be pro-Malay rather than pro-Chinese. The reason for this is not difficult to understand. The British were impressed by the inherent good manners and courtesy of the Malays especially when compared with the rather more brusque attitude of the immigrant Chinese labourers, although the British may sometimes have incorrectly interpreted Malay deference and politeness as evidence of weakness and lack of resolution.

Moreover, the Malay language or at least a working knowledge of it sufficient for everyday use, is not difficult to acquire and some of the British administrators, such as Frank Swettenham (afterwards Sir Frank Swettenham), Hugh Clifford (afterwards Sir Hugh Clifford), and William Maxwell (afterwards Sir William Maxwell), not to mention, in more recent times, Richard Winstedt (afterwards Sir Richard Winstedt), went far beyond this, and were among a select band of civil servants who acquired an excellent command of the language and were acknowledged to be Malay scholars.[9]

Malay households were open and friendly towards guests, and the Malays did not despise foreigners or, at least, display the xenophobia of the Chinese. Westerners were referred to by the harmless nickname of 'Mat Salleh' by Malays when they were talking among themselves, which somehow has a much more affectionate and tolerant ring about it than the ruder and more vulgar *ang mao* (Hokkien) or *hung mo kwai* (Cantonese), meaning 'red-haired devil', which was the equivalent Chinese expression.

It is true, too, that the British found the Chinese much more difficult to administer. They were tough, industrious, clever and independent, with little respect for westerners, especially as they were not impressed by the conduct of the latter in China, where they were regarded as 'pirates' and 'barbarians'. Nevertheless, the

British did obtain the cooperation of the Chinese headmen or *capitans* in Malaya in dealing with their own people, and usually this system of 'like governing like'[10] worked to the mutual advantage of both sides.

From 1877 onwards, when the Chinese Protectorate was established in Singapore under William Pickering, a British official who was fluent in several Chinese dialects, the British government, for the first time, was able to exercise a much more direct control over the Chinese.[11] Before that, the Chinese had been left largely to their own devices, and virtually allowed to govern themselves as an *imperium in imperio* through their own social, economic and political groupings, in which their secret societies played a very significant part. By and large, although it may not have been realized at the time, the Chinese *capitans,* through whom the British dealt with the Chinese, were in fact the secret society leaders.

It was the official British policy to preserve the use of the indigenous forms and institutions of the Malays, and to be solicitous of their views, in keeping with the philosophy that colonial rule was a form of trusteeship for the Malays, with the British acting as an 'umpire' mainly to keep the alien Chinese at bay and to look after the special interests of the Malays. When the British entered into treaties with the Malay rulers, they recognized the principle that the 'special rights' of the sultans and their Malay subjects must be protected. Looking ahead, it was these rights which were also recognized in the Federation of Malaya Agreement of 1948, and became the 'legal' basis for the New Economic Policy (NEP) incorporated in the *Second* and *Third Malaysia Plans,*[12] which will be touched upon later in this narrative.

The 'special position' of the Malay rulers and their Malay subjects was adverted to time and time again by the British administrators, and in an important speech delivered before the Federal Council in 1927, Sir Hugh Clifford, High Commissioner of the FMS, described the position of the rulers as sacrosanct and said there could be no yielding to the demands of aliens for democracy even though they had a majority, as this would represent a betrayal of the Malays.[13]

'These States were, when the British Government was invited by their Rulers and Chiefs to set their troubled houses in order, Muhammadan monarchies,' Clifford said. 'Such they are today, and such they must continue to be. No mandate has ever been extended to us by Rajas, Chiefs, or people to vary the system of government which has existed in these territories from time immemorial.... The adoption of any kind of government by majority would forthwith entail the complete submersion of the indigenous population, who would find themselves hopelessly outnumbered by the folk of other races; and this would produce a situation which would amount to a betrayal of trust which the Malays of these States, from the highest to the lowest, have been taught to repose in his Majesty's Government.'[14]

In the following year, W.G.A. Ormsby Gore, Parliamentary Under-Secretary for the Colonies, in a report covering his visit to Malaya in 1928, echoed Clifford's comments and said, 'Our position in every state rests on solemn treaty obligations ... [the States] were, are and must remain "Malay" States and the primary object of our share in the administration of these countries must always be the progress of the indigenous Malay inhabitants .... To me the maintenance of the position, authority and prestige of the Malay rulers is a cardinal point of policy.'[15]

At 'field level', a similar, if less elegantly worded view, had already been expressed exactly one hundred years earlier by the British Resident in Malacca, to the following effect:

'The improvement of their [i.e. Malay] condition and the progressive amelioration of the habits of the indigenous population must at all times be considered the great end of British Administration, and whatever may be the supposed advantages resulting from the introduction of Chinese or other foreign adventurers, the Governor in Council is satisfied that they are so dearly purchased by the exclusion, depression and degradation of the Original Malay Inhabitants of the Peninsula, who are in the first instance entitled to our protection and encouragement.'[16]

To revert to the main thread of our narrative, in 1909, Sir John Anderson, the then High Commissioner, expressed concern over the problem of 'over-centralization' under the federal system, that is, the pushing aside of both the sultans and the state councils, and admitted that the Malay rulers had been largely ignored and had lost considerably more of their power and authority than they had bargained for. 'They are confident,' he said, referring to the sultans, 'that we will never forget that our powers are derived wholly from their gift and that we are here in a Malay country as the advisers and counsellors of its Malay sovereigns'.[17] As a result of these considerations, an Agreement for the Constitution of a

Federal Council was drawn up in 1909 and signed by the Malay rulers. It was hoped that the Federal Council would, in principle, by bringing the Malay sultans into the inner machinery of the federation and giving them seats on the council, increase their authority, but in fact it did not prove to be a success as the power of the Resident-General in Kuala Lumpur remained undiminished.

In 1925, Sir Lawrence Guillemard, High Commissioner 1920—7, reverted to the invidious position of the Malay sultans, and mooted the idea of a policy of 'decentralization' which would preserve the individuality of the Malay states, and devolve more power to the Malay rulers.[18] This was vigorously opposed by Chinese and British unofficial members of the Federal Council, and by planters, who were in favour of retaining central control. The real crux of the matter was that they did not have confidence in the ability of the Malay states to provide an efficient administration without the continuing control and guidance of the British colonial power.

The decentralization debates of 1925—7 exposed a fundamental dilemma for Malaya. The issues were whether to build a modern unified state or to bolster the existing small Malay states, and it was eventually decided to follow the latter course.[19]

The Chinese point of view was different and it was put very succinctly by Tan Cheng Lock, a wealthy *baba* Chinese leader, whose family had been settled in Malacca for the past two hundred years, when he proposed in the Straits Settlements Legislative Council in 1926, that the aim should be a 'united self-governing British Malaya'.[20] In a memorandum touching on decentralization which he submitted to the Parliamentary Under-Secretary for the Colonies in 1936, he expressed the view that under decentralization, the FMS would be placed on very much the same constitutional basis as the UMS, and a small representation would be given on the various state councils to Chinese, European and Indian members, who would be 'decidedly and effectually outnumbered and overwhelmed by the British Resident and the Malay Sultan and his Chiefs who will constitute the bulk of the Council'.[21] He was disturbed by the idea that a powerful state council dominated by Malays and a pro-Malay British Resident would be in a position to shape the land, education and other policies to the disadvantage of the non-Malays. He expressed his disquiet, too, over 'discrimination against non-Malays', in that preference was given to Malays for employment in the government service. With regard to the government's education policy, he pointed out that free education was only given in the Malay vernacular while the government contributed hardly anything towards the maintenance of Chinese vernacular schools.[22] More will be said on these two points later.

Although Guillemard expressed satisfaction shortly before he retired in 1927 at the progress which had been made towards decentralization, in actuality very little had been accomplished, and as Emerson aptly put it, after Guillemard's departure, the latter's decentralization policy was 'tucked away in a cubbyhole'.[23]

His successor, Clifford, was content to let 'sleeping dogs lie', although he made it quite clear that he favoured a pro-Malay policy. However, when Sir Cecil Clementi arrived in 1930 from Hong Kong, where he had been governor, to take over from Clifford as high commissioner, the whole issue of decentralization was revived on a broader basis. Clementi had built up a considerable reputation as an experienced and knowledgeable administrator of Chinese, but paradoxically the policies he adopted in Malaya did not endear him to the Chinese. Essentially, his proposals were to make the FMS as similar as possible to the UMS, so that the latter would have no objection to a closer association. He wanted to streamline the administration of the country into a Malayan Union, to be made up of the FMS and the UMS, which he hoped the Straits Settlements and British Borneo would join later.[24]

It was intended that some services such as Agriculture, Education, Health, Mining and Public Works, Co-operatives, and Forestry should be transferred to state control, while some central services such as Railways, Customs, Posts and Telegraphs should be retained under federal control. The FMS were to receive two-fifths of the available revenue, and the post of Chief Secretary in Kuala Lumpur (which more or less corresponded to the former office of Resident-General, although it had been downgraded) should be redesignated Federal Secretary and made subordinate to the British Residents of the FMS who, in turn, it was envisaged, would become more like the Advisers in the UMS.[25]

However, the plan ran into considerable and widespread opposition from Chinese and western commercial interests, as had Guillemard's previously. The Malays, on the other hand, welcomed it as offering greater scope for Malay rule and weakening the centralized British control from Kuala Lumpur. Ironically, the sultans in the UMS were hostile because they were suspicious of British motives and they envisaged decentralization as leading to greater control from Singapore.[26]

The Malay point of view, however, was quite uncompromising, and it was crystallized in an article in a Malay journal, a translation of which appeared in the *Malay Mail* dated 12 November 1931, which said *inter alia* '... The Malay Peninsula belongs to the Malays. Our right is indisputable. It will remain so as long as we are fit to guard, control, and manage it.'

In 1932, Brigadier-General Sir Samuel Wilson, Under-Secretary for the Colonies, came out to Malaya to investigate the situation for himself. His official report was very comprehensive and diplomatic, and his finding was that from a purely economic viewpoint it was desirable to have a central government but from a political viewpoint, decentralization was the answer.[27] Nevertheless, the process of decentralization was to be gradual and at a much slower pace than had been visualized by Clementi.[28]

Chapter Three

Population Growth and Social Change: Chinese and Malays

Clementi's governorship was a turbulent one, and it was plagued with such problems as decentralization; the downturn of the economy due to the Great Depression (1929–32); the growing power of Chinese political societies in Malaya; the realization, which came as something of a shock, that the Malays were outnumbered for the first time in their own country by the non-Malays, and that something had to be done to control Chinese immigration; and the underlying and growing friction between Malays and Chinese.

At the time of Sir Samuel Wilson's mission to Malaya in 1932 to investigate the decentralization issue, the two opposing rallying slogans of 'Malaya for the Malays', which represented the feeling expressed in the Malay magazine article referred to earlier, and 'Malaya for the Malayans', which represented the Chinese and Indian stand, were heard for the first time. The term 'Malayan' in this context was taken to mean all locally born and domiciled people regardless of their ethnic group. A number of documents which summed up the fears and hopes of the Chinese in Malaya, were submitted to Wilson, during his stay in Malaya, by Tan Cheng Lock, Lai Tai Loke (another prominent Chinese community leader), the Associated Chinese Chambers of Commerce in Malaya, and the Perak Chinese community.

Tan Cheng Lock spoke for the Chinese community in the Straits Settlements Legislative Council in October 1932: '[The] Government has no fixed and constructive policy to win over the Straits and other Malayan-born Chinese, who are subjects of the country, and foster and strengthen their spirit of patriotism and natural love for the country of their birth and adoption,' he said. 'I look in vain for any tangible sign or indication of any active interest, practical sympathy and encouragement that has been shown by the Government of late years .... One is driven to the conclusion that the Bill is part and parcel of an anti-Chinese policy, probably with a political objective, based on distrust and fear, which the Chinese on the whole as a community have done nothing and have given absolutely no cause to merit.'[1]

The Bill that Tan Cheng Lock was referring to was enacted as the Aliens Ordinance 1933, and it was the outcome of Clementi's concern that the Malays were outnumbered 44.7 to 53.2 per cent by the Chinese and Indians, as brought out by the 1931 Census (see Appendix 2), and Clementi said that it was essential for the Malay rulers to formulate a 'policy for the immigrant races'.[2] He advocated not only the placing of restrictions on the entry of Chinese immigrants, but also a much stricter control over Chinese who were already in the country.

In the UMS, with the exception of Johore, which was affected by the forces of modernization in Singapore, the pace of development was slow, and they had a much more Malay character about them than the FMS. Yet, in the FMS, which apart from Pahang were on the west side of the peninsula where the main economic transformation was taking place, the Malays were in a greater minority, and the 1931 Census brought out that they were outnumbered 34.7 to 63.7 per cent by the non-Malays, as the following bar chart will indicate:[3]

1931 Census

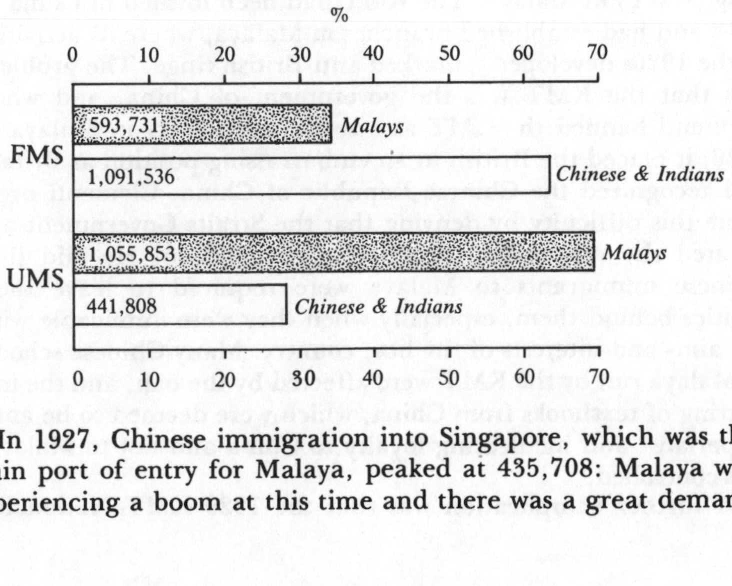

In 1927, Chinese immigration into Singapore, which was the main port of entry for Malaya, peaked at 435,708: Malaya was experiencing a boom at this time and there was a great demand for labour which the Malays were unwilling to meet. Moreover, it is probable that the troubled warlord period in China provided an added stimulus to Chinese immigration.[4] During the period of the Great Depression, however, Chinese immigration fell sharply and, for instance, in 1932 282,779 Chinese left Malaya to return to China against only 32,9[illegible]5 arrivals, and it did not rise again until just before the Japanese invasion of 1941.[5]

So, in fact, the Aliens Ordinance 1933 was a case of 'shutting the stable after the horse had fled' but, nevertheless, together with the Immigration Restriction Ordinance of 1928, it marked a radical departure from the old policy of throwing Malaya open to all comers by imposing a quota of 1,000 per month for male Chinese immigrants.[6] The importance of the 1933 Ordinance was that it remained the law by which Chinese immigration was controlled up to the time of the Pacific War.

With reference to Tan Cheng Lock's speech in the Singapore Legislative Council, it should be noted that by 1931, 31 per cent of the Chinese in Malaya were local born as compared with 22 per cent in 1921, and clearly this group could no longer be treated as transient aliens. It therefore seemed reasonable to expect that they should be considered by the British authorities and the Malay sultans as 'Malayan Chinese', having a stake in their country of birth and adoption.

Clementi then addressed himself to suppressing the Kuomintang (KMT) in Malaya. The KMT had been formed in China in 1912 and had established branches in Malaya, where its activities in the 1920s developed a marked anti-British tinge. The problem was that the KMT was the government of China, and when Clementi banned the KMT as a subversive society in Malaya in 1930, it placed the British in an embarrassing position as Britain had recognized the Chinese Republic of China. Clementi overcame this difficulty by denying that the Straits Government advocated the suppression of Chinese nationalism. He said that Chinese immigrants to Malaya were required to leave their politics behind them, especially when they were inimicable with the aims and interests of the host country. Many Chinese schools in Malaya run by the KMT were affected by the ban, and the importing of textbooks from China, which were deemed to be anti-imperialist and inculcating loyalty to China and not to Malaya, was controlled.

A further complication was that the 1929 KMT Nationality

Law, by application of the principle of *jus sanguinis,* treated all Chinese living in Malaya, whether local born or not, as Chinese citizens. This had the effect of increasing the suspicions of the Malays towards the Chinese living in their midst, especially when their spokesmen were beginning to ask for political rights and a greater say in the running of the country. The split between the left and right wings of the KMT in 1927 introduced yet another element of discord in Malaya as it led to the development of communism in Malaya. Nevertheless, Chinese underground political activities in Malaya died down somewhat after the Sino-Japanese War began in 1937, when Chinese nationalist fervour was directed primarily against Japan.[7]

The widespread Chinese political activities in Malaya which were connected with events in China, but which nevertheless caused considerable local unrest, did not pass unnoticed by the Malays, and only served to increase Malay doubts about the sincerity of Chinese protestations of loyalty to Malaya.

The Great Depression (1929—32) caused economic disaster on a worldwide scale, and had very serious effects on tin and rubber which were the mainstay of the Malayan economy. Although the Malays were not affected by the large-scale retrenchment of staff which had to take place in both these industries, the overall effect of a slump in an integrated economy is cumulative. Money was in short supply, the wages of government employees were cut, and great hardship resulted among all sections of the population, not only among tin mine and rubber estate workers, but among workers in many other sectors of the economy too.

By this time, it was evident that the Chinese and the Indians already controlled the economic life of the country as the Malays lacked the opportunities to participate in modern economic life and preferred their subsistence economy. The rubber and tin industries were in the hands of non-Malays (see Appendix 3), and the bulk of employees in commercial undertakings as well as most of the petty traders and craftsmen, were Chinese and Indians.[8] By the time of the Great Depression, it was abundantly clear that the Malays had become economically dispossessed in their own land, and although the policy of decentralization did to some extent enable them to retain political control, some of the more far-sighted Malays already perceived that the Chinese were beginning to pose a challenge to their political primacy. Many, indeed, felt that the British had not looked after Malay interests as well as they might have done, and that the Malays would have to assert themselves more forcibly to make sure that they were not overrun by the non-Malays, in particular, the Chinese.

However, as it transpired, the Great Depression was turned to the advantage of the Malays as, although a considerable retrenchment of government staff became necessary, wherever possible the policy followed was to retain Malays and dispense with non-Malay employees. Also, in those cases where in the interests of economy local officers were substituted for the more highly paid Europeans, preference was given to Malays.

When Perak, Selangor, Negri Sembilan and Pahang were federated as the FMS in 1896, the four separate state civil services were welded together to form the Malayan Civil Service (MCS). Recruitment to the MCS was by open competitive examination in London, but it was noteworthy that in 1910, recruitment had been restricted to natural-born British subjects of European descent.[9]

This policy effectively barred the recruitment of Asians into the higher ranks of the government administration service in Peninsular Malaya, but in 1933, Clementi established a Straits Settlements Civil Service, that is, a completely separate body from the MCS, which opened certain of the more junior administrative appointments in the Straits Settlements to 'locally-born Asiatic British subjects'.[10]

The position in the FMS was that while the sultans refused to allow non-Malays to hold senior posts in the government, they were not opposed to Chinese and Indians being appointed to technical posts if there was no Malay candidate available to fill them, provided that the ruler agreed, and 'the applicant had been born and had lived all his life in Malaya and his father had served the country well'.[11]

With the opening up of the Malay Peninsula in the late 1890s and the early 1900s, there was a tremendous expansion of European staff in the administrative and specialist branches of government, which was accompanied by an increase in the number of subordinate staff employed as clerks and technical workers. The majority of the junior staff were Chinese, Indians and Eurasians, with the Indians predominating in the Public Works, Post and Telegraphs, and Railway Departments. From the mid-1890s onwards, many senior British officials felt remiss at not employing more Malays in the junior ranks of government service, and as it was realized that employment in government depended on an education in English, increased opportunities were offered to Malays to gain entry to English schools with a view to their being employed as clerks and interpreters.[12]

Sir William Treacher, who was Resident-General of the FMS between 1902—4, said that the British were morally obliged to afford the Malays a prominent part in government and the development of their country,[13] which, of course, was in keeping with the 'special position' of the Malays under the Residential System.

The broad policy followed to implement this programme was to make available free vernacular education to the Malay peasantry, although it was of poor quality and had little developmental value, and, at the same time, to provide English education for a selected number of sons of the Malay elite to prepare them for more senior posts in government service.[14] The elitist Malay College, established in 1909 in Kuala Kangsar, which was run along the lines of a British public school, became the main English-medium school used to produce a cadre of English-educated young Malays for appointment to the Malay Administrative Service (MAS), which came into existence in 1910 as a junior branch of the MCS. Non-Malays were not eligible to join this Service.

However, most English-medium schools were situated in the towns, and not in the countryside where the majority of the Malays lived. Some were government institutions and others grant-in-aid schools, established and maintained by missionary societies with a certain quantum of government aid. In theory they catered for children of different ethnic groups, but as the majority of pupils were non-Malay, they only served to divide the English-educated from the vernacular-educated.

From very early times, the Chinese community founded and financed their own schools which were outside the government system. There were no government Chinese-medium schools, and, in fact, Chinese schools were not brought under government inspection until 1920 and then only for political and not educational reasons. It was not until 1923 that Chinese schools became eligible for a nominal grant from the government.[15]

The rationale of government in providing education was that while education in the vernacular should be free for all Malay children as 'Malay is the *lingua franca* of the country', it was not thought necessary to provide education for 'the children of alien temporary population in their own language'.[16]

Thus, the development of a plural school system in Malaya

seriously exacerbated racial tensions, and the non-Malays considered that the British were following a pro-Malay policy in furtherance of their intention to build up 'Malaya for the Malays'.[17]

As a result of the large scale Chinese immigration into Malaya in the latter half of the nineteenth and the early part of the twentieth centuries, the whole demographic picture changed. The towns and urban centres became predominantly Chinese settlements, and Chinese farmers and agriculturalists spread out, too, to fill vacant spaces in rural areas. Aliens had always been entitled to hold land and the Malays soon came to fear that they would be driven off the land if this movement continued, and reduced to becoming tenants of western, Chinese and Indian landlords. Representations were therefore made to the colonial government that Malays should be afforded special protection to safeguard the land held by them under customary tenure to prevent its loss to non-Malays, which meant notably the Chinese, and the British created great Malay reservations in which land could only be alienated to Malays and must not be transferred out of Malay hands.

The first Malay Reservation Enactment was promulgated in the FMS in 1913 and similar legislation was enacted in the UMS between 1930 and 1941. The extent of the reservations can be gauged from the map given in Appendix 7.

However, non-Malays were allowed to retain land acquired before the various enactments were promulgated and, usually, to transfer their holding to other non-Malays, as well as to own land outside the Malay reservations.[18]

The official position was given in an unpublished report of the FMS Malay Reservations Committee in 1931 which stated: 'We do not hold that the protection of a backward peasantry is the sole or the chief object of the policy of reservation. The policy is territorial, and whatever the competitive capacity of the Malay may be he cannot, as a race, compete with the far more populous peoples of other races who are attracted to Malaya. It is a question of numbers. If the future of the Malay is to be assured, he must have room for expansion, and that requires land to be reserved.'[19]

The principle followed was based on the formula that in no state in the FMS should the ratio between cultivable area in Malay reservations and the whole cultivable area of a state fall below 60 per cent, although, as far as can be traced, no public announcement was made to this effect. But in some more densely populated states such as Selangor and Negri Sembilan not even 50 per cent of the cultivable land could be so allocated 'without cutting into either forest or other reserves or into lands alienated to members of other races'.[20]

While it is true that the original legislation made it impossible for a Malay to transfer reservation land to a non-Malay, it did not prevent his pledging the land as security for a loan or advance. This loophole permitted Chinese and Indian (*chettiar*) moneylenders and speculators to obtain effective control of the land, with the Malay remaining owner in name only.

In 1933, the Malay Reservation Enactment of the FMS was therefore amended to forbid charge or lease to a non-Malay, and similar laws were introduced in the other states.

Whereas the Malays regarded the reservations as necessary to protect their special rights as cultivators, the Chinese, on the other hand, looked upon them as just another example of the 'Malaya for the Malays' policy being followed by the British authorities. They felt it all the more acutely when it became apparent that for purposes of the enactment, the term 'Malay' was defined as 'a person belonging to any Malayan race who habitually speaks the Malay language, or any Malayan language, and who professes the Muslim religion'.[21] Immigrants from the Dutch East Indies came within this definition, no matter whether they were recent arrivals or not, but the Chinese were excluded whether they had been settled in Malaya for generations or had recently arrived from China.

Chapter Four

Sino-Malay Relations: The Japanese Occupation and British Reoccupation

Up to the time of the Japanese invasion of Malaya in December 1941, Malaya was still divided for administrative purposes into the Straits Settlements, the four Federated Malay States and the five Unfederated Malay States, and although Britain was the paramount power, the system of government was very cumbersome and unwieldy for a territory about the size of England. There was no political unity in Malaya nor common citizenship.

Persons born in the Straits Settlements, a British colony under direct British rule, were British subjects. On the other hand, the Malay States were protected states, and persons born in them were subjects of the particular Malay ruler.[1] There was no feeling of nationalism or over-riding Malayan loyalty. The Malays owed allegiance to their sultans, and thought of themselves as belonging to Selangor, Pahang, Kelantan, and so on, rather than to Malaya. British policy was, broadly speaking, anti-Chinese and pro-Malay.[2]

Meanwhile, educated Malays were becoming increasingly frustrated with the fact that, despite the pro-Malay policy adopted by the British, the Chinese still dominated Malaya's economic life. They were concerned, too, at the growing numerical strength and power of the Chinese, and the stirrings of Chinese political consciousness as expressed, for instance, in the views of Tan Cheng Lock, the Straits-born Chinese leader, who advocated a 'united self-governing Malayan nation', in which locally-domiciled Chinese would be given equal rights with Malays. Other Chinese leaders were more assertive, and a Chinese legislative councillor addressing a Chinese association in 1931 said, referring to Malaya, 'This is ours, our country'.[3] Clearly, opinions of this nature were, to say the least, untactful and not conducive to placating Malay feelings, and they undoubtedly only helped to increase the growing tension between the two communities.

According to the 1931 Census, 38 per cent of the Chinese in the Straits Settlements and 31 per cent in Malaya were local born. The Chinese were no longer content to be treated as aliens. They looked for citizenship rights and other privileges which went with domicile, and they resented the immigration restrictions of the 1930s which they felt were aimed primarily at themselves. Most of all, they felt uneasy about their position under the 'Malaya for the Malays' policy being followed by the British.[4]

At this juncture, the Japanese invaded Malaya, and a curtain descended on British rule for the next three and a half years. In a lightning campaign which lasted only two and a half months, the Japanese army swept the British before them in their drive down the Malay Peninsula from the north, and Singapore capitulated on 15 February 1942.

From the start, the Japanese recognized that communal differences existed between the main ethnic groups constituting Malaya, that is, the Malays, the Chinese and the Indians, and that there was no united nationalist movement against British rule which could be exploited. Malaya and Sumatra were administered as one unit under the command of the Japanese 25th Army, which seemed to give a more Indonesian-Malay slant to Malaya. Although the Japanese did not recognize the status of the Malay rulers at the onset and intended that they should be made to 'dedicate their land and people to the Japanese',[5] their policy changed in November 1942, and the sultans were recognized in the same way as they had been by the British. Throughout, however, the Japanese were suspicious of the Chinese, especially in view of the stiff Chinese resistance they had encountered in the Sino-Japanese conflict which had started in 1937, and the fierce struggle put up by Chinese communist and other volunteer units used by the British during the closing stages of the battle for Singapore.[6]

The Malays were thrown onto themselves, especially as they were deprived of the protecting power of the British. In some ways, they were not as anti-Japanese as the Chinese, and many of them undoubtedly hoped that the Japanese would be able to deal with the Chinese for them and 'keep them in their place'.

One of the first steps the Japanese took was to release from custody the leaders of the Association of Malay Youths *(Kesatuan Melayu Muda)* (KMM), who had been detained by the British under the wartime Defence Regulations.[7] The KMM's aims embraced independence for Malaya and union with Indonesia. It believed that the two countries shared a common destiny and had common historical, cultural and religious bonds. It was pro-Islam and anti-Chinese in its outlook.[8]

The British had actually intended to fly the KMM leader, Ibrahim bin Ya'acob, who was the top Malay nationalist, to India and to intern him there but he was still under detention in Singapore when it fell to the Japanese. Even though the Japanese banned the KMM, as they probably realized the danger of such undercover movements, they soon released Ibrahim and appointed him to command a Japanese-sponsored Malay army referred to as Defenders of the Motherland *(Pembela Tanah Ayer)* (PETA) *(Giyugun* in Japanese), with the rank of lieutenant-colonel.

Under the Japanese, the way was clear, now that the British had gone, for Malays to occupy senior posts in government service, which they would not have had the chance of doing under British rule, thus enabling them to gain valuable experience in administering the country. These Malay elitists became more politically oriented and provided the leadership for postwar Malay political activities.[9]

The Japanese encouraged the concept of *Indonesia Raya* (Greater Indonesia), which envisaged the amalgamation of Indonesia and Malaya as one political unit, and while they were not keen on granting Malaya independence itself, the impression was given that when Indonesia was granted independence (the Japanese considered it to be more politically advanced than Malaya), Malaya would become independent too.[10]

Once the Japanese collapse seemed imminent, the Japanese decided, in July 1945, only a few weeks before surrendering, to accelerate their plans to grant Indonesia independence. At a meeting attended by the Secretary-Generals of the Military Administration of Java, Sumatra, the Celebes and Malaya towards the end of that month, a new party known as *Kesatuan Ra'ayat Indonesia Semenanjong* (People's Association of the Indonesian Peninsula) (KRIS), emerged under the leadership of Ibrahim Ya'acob, with the aim of encouraging the idea of *Indonesia Raya,* and generally promoting the concept of Malay nationalism. The acronym KRIS chosen for this party was particularly apt as it formed the Malay word for the traditional dagger with a wavy blade which is common to both the Malay and Indonesian languages.[11]

On 12 August, Ibrahim Ya'acob had an unscheduled meeting with Sukarno and Dr Hatta, the Indonesian leaders, at Taiping airport, at a brief stopover the latter two leaders made on their return to Jakarta from a meeting with Field Marshal Count Terauchi, the Japanese Regional Commander for Southeast Asia, at Dalat in Indo-China, and it is reliably reported that Ibrahim discussed the *Indonesia Raya* plan with them.[12]

However, the programme for the joint independence of Indonesia and Malaya, and the formation of *Indonesia Raya,* was thrown out of gear by the sudden Japanese surrender two days later on 14 August 1945. When Sukarno proclaimed Indonesia's independence on 17 August, he made no mention of Malaya, although it is known that he himself and several other Indonesian nationalists, such as Mohammad Yamin, were in favour of the inclusion of Malaya and the former British territories of Borneo, within the boundaries of the Republic of Indonesia. It seems likely that this was because Dr Hatta counselled a more cautious approach, but in any case Sukarno may have felt that he had quite enough on his hands in dealing with the problems of Indonesian independence without compounding them by taking over Malaya's as well.[13]

Meanwhile, KRIS went ahead with its scheduled Congress in Kuala Lumpur on 16 and 17 August. In passing, it is interesting to note that one of the original members of KRIS, and a participant at the Congress, was Dato Onn bin Ja'afar, the father of Datuk Hussein Onn, who later became prime minister of Malaysia. Dato Onn subsequently founded the United Malays National Organization (UMNO), which will figure prominently in this account in due course.

The plan for Malaya's independence and union with Indonesia had obviously misfired, but it was resolved at the KRIS Congress to continue with the nationalist struggle in Malaya. Ibrahim himself did not attend the meeting, but flew to Jakarta from Singapore on 19 August, where he assumed another name and passed from history.[14]

When the British occupation forces arrived in Malaya in late September 1945, the KMM, PETA and KRIS leaders were arrested but they were later released. Although KRIS was dissolved, its mantle was assumed by the Malay Nationalist Party (MNP), which became active in the political arena early on after the British return, with its central aim a Malaya-Indonesia union. The British authorities banned the MNP and all other left-wing Malay political parties soon after 1948, when the Emergency Regulations were announced.

By the time the British returned to Malaya in September 1945, the Japanese occupation of Malaya had lasted three and a half years, and the entire population had suffered grievously during this period, particularly because the cessation of rice imports led to widespread malnutrition.[15] The Chinese, in particular, had been treated terribly. Thousands were killed in purges carried out by the Japanese during the first days of the occupation, and many more fled to the interior of Malaya where they became squatters on the jungle fringes. By the time British rule was re-established, the country had been brought to the verge of an economic breakdown, and the policy of divide and rule which the Japanese had followed, favouring the Malays against the Chinese, only had the effect of intensifying underlying racial animosities.

The ill-feeling which had been generated in this way resulted in the outbreak of serious Sino-Malay riots in the *inter-regnum* period of about a month between the surrender of the Japanese and the return of the British.

During the war, anti-Japanese guerilla activities had been carried out by the Malayan People's Anti-Japanese Army (MPAJA), which was almost entirely Chinese and under the control of the Malayan Communist Party, while the civilian supporters of the MPAJA, again almost entirely Chinese, were organized as the Malayan People's Anti-Japanese Union (MPAJU). In general, the Malays tended to be cooperative with, or at least obedient to, Japanese rule, although there were a few Malay anti-Japanese guerilla groups, such as the *Wataniah* in Pahang.[16]

During this twilight period, the MPAJA took the law into its own hands in meting out summary justice to those people (mostly Malays) who were suspected of collaborating with the Japanese. The Malays reacted to this by attacking Chinese. In the interior of Negri Sembilan, for instance, Malays set upon and slaughtered forty Chinese villagers, mostly women and children. In retaliation, Chinese assailed Malays living along the Perak River.[17]

Meanwhile, in preparation for the return of the British to Malaya, the Eastern Department of the British Colonial Office had been active in drawing up plans for a radically different

Malayan constitution, which was the Malayan Union, to rationalize, streamline and unify the administration of Malaya, and to introduce a common citizenship to satisfy the claims of non-Malays for a share of responsibility in the government of the country. However, before dealing with this development, we should glance at what had been taking place outside Malaya during the Japanese occupation, which has a bearing on the theme of Sino-Malay relations.

Tan Cheng Lock and his family succeeded in obtaining passages on a ship leaving Singapore for India about a month before the fall of Singapore, and they remained in India during the war, together with a large number of other refugees from Malaya.[18] In December 1942, a Malayan Association of India was formed, with Tunku Abu Bakar, a prince of the Johore royal house, as patron, and a committee consisting mostly of Europeans with some prominent Singapore Jews and Straits Chinese. More than two-thirds of the Malayan refugees joined this Association, which submitted a memorandum to the Colonial Office in London offering its help in the post-war reconstruction of Malaya. The Chinese members were not happy that the Association was dominated by Europeans, and they broke away in November 1943 to establish the Overseas-Chinese Association in Bombay, with Tan Cheng Lock as chairman.

Tunku Abu Bakar described this as 'Chinese preparing to dabble in Malayan politics'.[19]

In November 1943, Tan Cheng Lock wrote to the Secretary of State for the Colonies to request that the Chinese community of Malaya should be represented on any committee formed for the reconstruction and reoccupation of Malaya, and to offer his Association's assistance and cooperation.[20]

Tan Cheng Lock forwarded with his letter a 'Memorandum on the Future of Malaya', which is a very interesting document as it indicates the way in which the Malayan-Chinese were thinking about Malaya. After pointing out that in 1940, the Chinese (2,400,000) and the Indians (750,000) combined outnumbered the Malays (2,300,000), Tan Cheng Lock went on to say that not more than one half of the Malay population was indigenous and the rest was made up of immigrant 'Malaysians' from the Netherlands East Indies, who were not actually Malays. The Malayan government, he continued, 'should make it its fundamental policy and aim to foster amity and harmony among the principal races ... which make up its composite population, to all racial elements in which equal rights, political, economic and otherwise should be accorded, so as to build up a Malayan community with Malayan consciousness and inspired by Malayan patriotism ....'[21]

He advocated self-government and the framing of a new post-war constitution for Malaya with rights of representation in the Legislative Assembly and the Government of Malaya to be apportioned between Malays, Chinese and other races in the ratio of 3, 2 and 1 respectively, which accorded with the population figures of the various communities concerned. Even this representation did not concede, he continued, the measure of representation to the Chinese to which they were entitled by their economic importance and the amount of public revenue contributed by them. He emphasized the heroic stand made by Chinese communists and the Chinese volunteers, largely recruited from the China-born Chinese community, in the defence of Singapore, as evidence of their potential loyalty as citizens, and recommended that the best way to treat the Chinese was to trust them and to give those who had become domiciled for a sufficiently long period the opportunity to acquire Malayan citizenship by naturalization. In post-war Malaya, the imposing of immigration restrictions on Chinese for political reasons should cease. Irrespective of race, every community domiciled in Malaya should be encouraged to regard itself as Malayan. Dealing with the economic aspect, and the special position of the Malays, Tan Cheng Lock said: 'While it is necessary that the Malays, [who are more backward *(sic)* than the other races], should be protected against unfair competition and exploitation, especially in relation to their tenure of lands for agricultural purposes and in their home villages, and should be assisted by the Government in every way to accelerate their economic and educational advancement and progress in other respects, the interests and rights of the other races should not thereby be affected to their detriment and in such a way as to hamper their development and advancement.'[22]

Further memoranda were submitted by other bodies indicating their views on the post-war reconstruction of Malaya, but Tan Cheng Lock's is the only one giving such a concise picture of Malayan-Chinese views.

Mention should be made, however, of detailed proposals sent to Britain in February 1943 by Tunku Mahmud Mahydeen, a prince of the Kelantan royal house, who had been Director of Education in Kelantan at the time of the Japanese invasion and who had escaped to India, as these proposals are indicative of a Malay point of view. Mahydeen recommended the unification of Malaya and the abolition of the Malay rulers. He was prepared to accept domiciled immigrants as citizens but he proposed that further Chinese and Indian immigration to Malaya should be stopped and that Javanese should be encouraged to immigrate instead, as it would be much easier to assimilate them into Malay society. He regarded a knowledge of Malay as a *sine qua non* for the acquisition of Malayan citizenship, and he indicated that he was in favour of increased educational facilities for Malays to enable them to improve their position in society.

The Colonial Office welcomed Mahydeen's views for a united Malaya with common citizenship as they fitted in with its own plans, and it wished to weaken the power of the rulers, but it did not accept his suggestions dealing with immigration, the promotion of the Malay language, and the extension of educational privileges to the Malays.[23]

The Malayan Union Scheme, drafted in Britain during the war by the Colonial Office, was established barely six months after the British reoccupation of Malaya. Sir Harold MacMichael, who was entrusted with the task of negotiating it with the rulers, arrived in October 1945. By December 1945, he had met all nine Malay rulers and had obtained their agreement to the new proposals. The Malayan Union was not a federal association, but a highly centralized union, which was a complete reversal of British policy before the Japanese occupation. It was made up of all the Malay states, together with Penang and Malacca. Singapore was excluded on account of its strategic importance to Britain, and because its inclusion would have tilted the racial balance in favour of the Chinese.

The Malayan Union was probably seen by the British as the first step in the long journey leading to Malayan independence. It represented a virtual annexation of the Malay states, and the reduction of the status of the Malay rulers to that of mere religious figureheads, which the Malays regarded as a tremendous blow to their esteem and self-respect. There were to be no state governments but only a central government in Kuala Lumpur under a British governor. There was to be a Pan-Malayan education department in Kuala Lumpur, and English was to be used as a common language to foster inter-racial harmony. Primary education was to be in the vernacular, but the medium of instruction in all secondary schools was to be English.[24] The assets of the nine Malay states and the Settlements of Penang and Malacca were to be transferred to the central government. The greatest threat to the Malay position was posed, however, by the new citizenship proposals, as non-Malays were to be eligible for Malayan Union citizenship if they had been born in Malaya or had resided there for ten out of the preceding fifteen years. It was estimated that on this basis, 83 per cent of the Chinese and 75 per cent of the Indians in Malaya would qualify for citizenship. It was intended to open the civil service in the Malay states to non-Malays and thus change what had previously been the preserve of the Malays and the British.[25]

Malay reaction to the scheme was unexpectedly serious and widespread, and it led to the Menteri Besar of Johore Dato Onn bin Ja'afar's forming the United Malays National Organization (UMNO) in March 1946 to lead the massive Malay opposition to the scheme. UMNO relied on the power structure of traditional Malay society, and former high commissioners and other senior Malayan civil servants, such as Sir Frank Swettenham, Sir Cecil Clementi, Sir George Maxwell, and Sir Richard Winstedt, living in retirement in Britain, gave their support to its cause.[26] Curiously, non-Malays initially remained apathetic although the Malayan Union proposals improved their position and gave them political rights which they had been denied previously, and there was every reason why they should resist opposition to them.

The UMNO case was based on what it referred to as an illegal transfer by *force majeure* of sovereign rights from the Malay rulers to the British Crown. The Malays said that MacMichael had forced the rulers to sign the new agreements by threatening to depose them, if they refused to do so, for 'collaborating' with the Japanese. UMNO sought the reaffirmation of the authority and prestige of the rulers and the acceptance of the fundamental principle that Malaya was a Malay country (*tanah Melayu*), and that the non-Malays were guests in it. Therefore, any concessions granted to non-Malays would be at the sole discretion of the Malays, who held the political power.[27]

As far as Chinese claims for equal political rights were concerned, the UMNO view was that they could be given consideration only when the Malays had attained economic parity with the

Chinese. The Malays felt it was absolutely necessary for them to keep political power in their hands in order to protect themselves from being swamped by the non-Malays. They were still suspicious, too, of the interest being shown by the Chinese Nationalist government in China in the Malayan Chinese. Under the 1929 Nationality Law based on the principle of *jus sanguinis,* the Chinese Nationalist government took the view that all Malayan Chinese were Chinese nationals, and this was used by the Malays to cast doubt on the sincerity of the Chinese in Malaya in desiring Malayan citizenship.[28]

Another factor which undoubtedly increased the suspicion of the Malays was the increased activity of the Malayan Communist Party (MCP), most of whose members were Chinese.

As a result of the UMNO-led opposition to the Malayan Union, in July 1946 the British agreed to form a Working Committee composed of six government and two UMNO representatives and four representatives of the Malay rulers, which was presided over by Malcolm MacDonald, British Commissioner-General for Southeast Asia, to draft an alternative constitution.[29]

This committee eventually agreed to a new constitution, which was then passed to non-Malay representatives for comment, and after its adoption, the short-lived Malayan Union was replaced by the Federation of Malaya on 1st February 1948. It is interesting to note that the constitution of the Federation of Malaya is the basis of Malaysia's constitution today. The Malays had won their case. The Federation of Malaya Agreement stated that the high commissioner would be responsible for safeguarding the 'special position' of the Malays and the 'legitimate interests' of the non-Malays.[30] Meanwhile, important issues that were to dominate Malayan politics up to the present, such as the special rights and privileges of the Malays, the position of the Malay rulers, and the place of the Chinese in Malaya, had been aired and brought out into the open.

In essence, the Federal Agreement was an Anglo-Malay compromise, as the Chinese were excluded from the Working Committee, although their views were sought before the Agreement became law.[31] The MacMichael Treaties were cancelled. The Malay rulers were recognized as sovereign monarchs, which meant that constitutionally the *Persekutuan Tanah Melayu* (Federation of Malaya) was a Malay state. It will be remembered that UMNO sought the recognition of Malaya as a Malay country (*tanah Melayu*) (see p. 32), and the inclusion of this term in the official Malay version of the name of the Federation was, therefore, significant.

The nine states and their rulers were to retain certain definite powers, that is, 'the prerogatives, power and jurisdiction which they enjoyed prior to the Japanese occupation'.[32] The British postwar policy of preparing Malaya for eventual self-government was continued and, under the scheme, a British high commissioner would govern the country with full powers.

The Malays accepted (as a concession on their part) a Federal citizenship which would be offered to those who owed undivided loyalty and allegiance to the Federation. But the qualifications for eligibility were considerably tightened up. For local-born applicants whose parents were immigrants, the residential period required was eight out of the preceding twelve years, and for foreign-born applicants, fifteen of the preceding twenty-five. It was necessary to demonstrate an adequate knowledge of Malay or English. Subjects of the Malay rulers were automatically Federal citizens, so under these arrangements virtually all Malays and Indonesian settlers qualified for Federal citizenship.[33]

In 1950, there were 3,275,000 Federal citizens, of which 2,500,000 or 76.33 per cent were Malays and only about 500,000 or 15.26 per cent Chinese.[34] The stringent birth qualification, the language test and the lengthy residential terms barred most of the non-Malays from becoming citizens.

The majority of Malays were satisfied with the new constitution but the Chinese did not think much of it, especially the exclusion of Singapore, which was predominantly a Chinese city, and the restrictive citizenship laws. The Chinese protested and launched a *hartal,* and threatened to walk out of the various councils. They were supported by some political parties, forming a united front known as the All-Malaya Council of Joint Action (AMCJA), which represented a rather belated non-Malay opposition to Malay nationalism.[35]

The president of the AMCJA was Tan Cheng Lock but as the AMCJA coalition did not have the cohesion of UMNO, it was unable to play a commanding role in the course of events, and it failed to achieve its purpose.[36]

Chapter Five

The Interplay of Sino-Malay Relations: The Emergency to Merdeka

In May 1948, five months after the formation of the Federation of Malaya, the country was in the grip of a growing lawlessness instigated by the Malayan Communist Party (MCP). Vast quantities of rubber were stolen, rubber estates were burnt down, and British rubber planters and tin miners were assassinated. It was clear by June that the government had a full-scale communist insurrection on its hands. A state of Emergency was declared on 18 June 1948, although the MCP and its subsidiary organizations were not officially banned until 23 July, and battle was joined between the Malayan People's Anti-British Army (MPABA) — the name was changed on 1 February 1949 to the Malayan Races Liberation Army (MRLA) — and the Malayan authorities, which was to last twelve years.[1]

It is difficult to say whether the decision to raise the standard of revolt was an internal MCP matter or whether it was influenced by pressures exerted by international communism. But a number of observers at the time, including Malcolm MacDonald, British Commissioner-General for Southeast Asia, were of the opinion that it was due to the latter reason.[2]

At a meeting of the Cominform in September 1947, communist parties throughout the world were exhorted to pursue a militant policy towards imperialism. This line was passed on to Southeast Asian communist parties and other front organizations at a meeting held in Calcutta in March 1948, and it is significant that a few months after this meeting communist uprisings started in Malaya, Burma, the Philippines and Hyderabad. Armed communist revolts had already broken out in Indonesia and Vietnam.[3]

The intention of the MCP in Malaya was to achieve a quick victory. The two basic industries of tin and rubber, which were the cornerstones of the Malayan economy, were to be destroyed, and then areas were to be occupied in the interior of Malaya which would be declared 'Liberated Areas', and finally, by joining up these 'Liberated Areas', a Democratic People's Republic of Malaya was to be established by August 1948.[4]

As far as Sino-Malay relations were concerned, the problem was that the vast majority of the members and supporters of the MCP were Chinese whereas the bulk of the security forces were British and Commonwealth troops, in support of the Malayan Police, which was overwhelmingly Malay. The struggle therefore lent itself to interpretation in racial terms, although this was never countenanced officially, as being primarily between Chinese communist guerillas, supported by the armed *Min Yuen* (People's Movement), which in terms of membership was almost entirely Chinese, and the Malays, supported by the British. The *Min Yuen* was the 'fifth column' of the MRLA which provided money, medical supplies, food and other material required by them.[5]

According to Malayan Police sources, the membership of the MCP at the time of the declaration of the Emergency was around 12,000 to 14,000, of whom ninety per cent were Chinese. Nevertheless, the MRLA probably never had many more than four to five thousand guerillas fighting in the jungle.[6]

In areas where the Malays predominated there was, generally speaking, an absence of communist activity. However, the MCP was successful in raising a Malay regiment in Pahang, with a few Indians in it, and there were some Malay terrorists in other parts of Malaya. Even so, the MCP attempt to broaden its base by claiming to be a nationalist movement (this was the reason for changing its name from MPABA to MRLA), with support from the three main Malayan communities, that is, Malays and Indians, as well as Chinese, never really succeeded.[7]

In addition to the *Min Yuen,* the MRLA relied on Chinese squatters for supplies and recruits. It became apparent that casualties inflicted on the MRLA by the security forces were quickly replaced by recruits from among the squatters. Most of the squatters, who have been referred to in Chapter Four above, were China-born Chinese who had moved out from towns and villages during the Second World War to avoid the attention of the Japanese. They lived very much as aliens, ran their own schools, and were resentful of interference by the authorities. By 1949, it was estimated that there were around half a million of them. As they lived on the jungle fringes outside effective British control, it was easy for the terrorists to prey upon them, and they came under communist domination, either voluntarily or involuntarily. The British authorities realized that something had to be done to cut off their contact with the MRLA.[8]

In June 1950, Lieutenant-General Sir Harold Briggs, Director of Operations in Malaya, and formerly of the Indian Army, began to put into action his plan to resettle squatters in 'new villages'. Under this scheme, which was spread over four years, about half a million squatters (85 per cent of whom were Chinese and the remainder mostly Malays) were moved into resettlement camps, mainly in the west coast states.

The government tried to ensure that each squatter family was provided with a means of livelihood such as, for instance, a thirty-year lease to a small plot of land which could be farmed, and that new villages had benefits such as electric light, water, schools, and community halls. But resettlement was fundamentally a military operation, which had to be carried out as quickly as possible, and very often what happened in practice did not accord with theory. Some of the squatters, for instance, were not adequately compensated for livestock which could not be moved to the new location, and sometimes personal belongings and various household fittings and furniture which could not be taken along had to be abandoned without adequate compensation or with no compensation at all. Title to vacant land was vested in the Malay ruler of the state, and frequently he did not relish the idea of alienating it to Chinese. The new villages were armed camps, with defensive positions around the perimeter, surrounded by barbed-wire fences, and guarded day and night by police. No one was allowed out at night, and in the morning, workers going out to work were subjected to a thorough body search to ensure that they were not carrying any supplies which could be passed on to the terrorists. But to look at the matter from another perspective, the resettlement programme was a vast undertaking involving the uprooting of one tenth of the population of Malaya (and one in every four of the Federation's Chinese population of two million) and, in the long run, it undoubtedly dealt a severe blow to the MRLA by disrupting its sources of supply.[9]

Nevertheless, in spite of the government's good intentions, resettlement left an underlying feeling among the Chinese that they had been singled out for unwelcome attention in this way (and reinforced their belief that the British administration was pro-Malay), and that they were being subjected to much more discomfort and hardship than the Malays. Many were bitter over what they regarded as forced resettlement in 'concentration camps'. Yet, on the other hand, the large expenditure on Chinese new villages was criticized by the Malays on the grounds that amenities in Malay *kampungs* were far inferior to what was provided in the new villages. They felt that 'a Chinese insurrection was bad enough without the additional insult of vast expenditure upon what they took to be an essentially alien community'.[10] The Malay rulers made it clear, too, that they were opposed to the idea of such large-scale Chinese resettlement in their states, as it would upset the sensitive Sino-Malay political balance.[11]

Meanwhile, developments were taking place in China which had a bearing on the struggle in Malaya. In the latter part of 1949, the Chinese communists drove the KMT out of China into exile in Taiwan, and the People's Republic of China was established. The British government was not long in recognizing the new regime. This had a marked effect on the Emergency in Malaya. The MCP was heartened by the turn of events, and felt that it was only a matter of time before the British would have to come to terms with them. The Chinese themselves were not certain who was going to win, especially in view of communist successes in other parts of Asia, and they became markedly less ready to cooperate with the government and more inclined to keep their options open. The MCP took full advantage of this fence-sitting and imposed a reign of terror on those Chinese who supported the government and many were murdered for providing information to the security forces or refusing to give assistance to the MCP. By 1951, for instance, there were only 1,500 Chinese in the Malayan Police which had an overall strength of 60,000,[12] and the lack of assistance which the Chinese community gave the security forces and the government caused serious concern to the British authorities. A serious information gap had grown up between the Malayan government and the Chinese community, as the Secretariat for Chinese Affairs had been abolished, and there were so few European officers who spoke Chinese, and hardly any Malays at all. Some of the wealthy Chinese community leaders were not averse to betting on both sides by paying extortion money to the MCP even though their own economic interests would obviously be affected if the MCP succeeded in overthrowing the Malayan government.[13]

On the political front, the Chinese leaders made it clear that they objected to the 'special position' of the Malays and the restricted rights of citizenship given to the Chinese under the constitution of the Federation of Malaya. They feared that if the British went ahead and granted Malaya self-government, the Malays would be dominant politically, and their own economic position would be threatened.[14]

Meanwhile, the government intensified its anti-terrorist operations and in November 1950 conscription for military or paramilitary service was introduced for Malayan youths between the ages of eighteen and twenty-four. This caused an outcry among the Chinese community. The Chinese press was most outspoken against the proposals, and Tan Cheng Lock explained that Chinese traditionally owed loyalty first and foremost to their family rather than to the nation, and asked for exemption for eldest and only sons.[15]

As the government was not prepared to give in to pressure and to modify its national service law, there was a mass exodus of Chinese youths to Singapore, Hong Kong and mainland China, and some went underground to join the MRLA.

During the next four years or so, the exodus to China of young Chinese whose aim was to serve the 'New China' and avoid military call-up in Malaya continued at a steady rate. After the communist successes in Indo-China in the first part of 1954, it was estimated that departures rose to an average of about one thousand per month.[16]

The Malay press was vociferous in passing stricture on the behaviour of the Chinese,[17] and these events only served to reinforce Malay doubts and misgivings about the Chinese in Malaya, in spite of the repeated protests of Chinese leaders such as Tan Cheng Lock that the Chinese in Malaya thought of Malaya as their home and the sole focus of their allegiance.[18]

It was against the backdrop of the Emergency, and the ebb and flow of military operations which culminated in the defeat of the terrorists and the lifting of the Emergency on 31 July 1960, when the remnants of the communist insurgents retreated into southern Thailand, that other important political developments affecting Sino-Malay relations began to take shape, which we shall now have to examine.

At the beginning of the Emergency in 1948, UMNO was already well-established, and it had built up a considerable following among the Malays, especially as a result of its determined stand against the short-lived Malayan Union. The Indian community in Malaya had established, too, the Malayan Indian Congress (MIC). It was only the Chinese who did not have a similar political grouping.

Sir Henry Gurney, High Commissioner of the Federation of Malaya, was anxious to encourage the formation of an organization among the Chinese which would be to all intents and purposes the equivalent of UMNO, and to develop a sense of involvement and belonging among the Chinese. Although there are several versions of the genesis of the Malayan Chinese Association (MCA), which was the party eventually formed by the Chinese, it is likely that the initiative was taken by Gurney in approaching Tan Cheng Lock.[19]

The MCA came into existence in February 1949, with Tan Cheng Lock as president. Membership was restricted to Chinese who intended to settle permanently in Malaya, and had either been born there or lived there for at least five years. Later it opened its membership to non-Chinese but this did not have much practical effect, and from the beginning it was clearly a Chinese communal party. Firstly, it was a 'welfare' body to raise funds to help with the resettlement of Chinese squatters in the new villages. Secondly, it hoped to vie with the MCP for the support of the poorer Chinese and, thirdly, to act as a mouthpiece for the Malayan Chinese community in asserting 'the indisputable claim of those of us who intend to settle down here permanently and make this country the object of their loyalty, to share fully and equally with the others the rights and privileges and the duties and responsibilities of Malayan citizenship.'[20]

In general, MCA policy was conciliatory toward the Malays and cooperative with the British authorities.

Both UMNO and MCA were communal parties, but their top leadership had common ground in that it was composed of English-educated Malay and Chinese elitists, representing the conservative elements of both communities, which did not rule out cooperation at this level.[21]

However, racial harmony and cooperation at ground level were still a long way off. One of the ways to bring about integration in a multiracial society is through education. After the Second World War the government policy was to reorganize the pre-war education system of having separate vernacular schools for

Malays, Chinese and Indians. It was recognized that the pre-war system only fostered a centrifugal tendency. In fact, only the approximate twenty per cent of the total student population in Malaya who attended English-medium schools came into contact with each other. A unified system of education was recommended by the Barnes Committee, which was set up to look into the system of Malay vernacular education, and the committee recommended that children of all races should attend national schools. The most important feature of the national primary schools was that they would be bilingual and all pupils would be taught English and Malay. The best students would then proceed to English-medium secondary schools. It was hoped that in this way a common nationality and outlook would be built up, especially as the syllabi would have a local Malayan slant.[22]

In 1951, Sir Henry Gurney appointed a committee, which was headed by Dr. W.P. Fenn and Dr. Wu Teh-yao, to investigate Chinese education in Malaya. The recommendations of this committee were quite different from those of the Barnes Report. While it was acknowledged that education should have a Malayan orientation, it was felt that a system of belonging could be inculcated by maintaining the different cultures and separate school systems of the main ethnic groups in Malaya.[23]

The conflicting views of the above two committees were studied by yet a third committee in 1951 and it was determined that the major point at issue, especially as far as the Chinese were concerned, was the formation of the national schools and the use of Malay and English as media of instruction.

As a result, the Education Ordinance promulgated in 1952, which covered the above features, was in a sense a compromise. Although insisting that national schools should be the pattern to be followed, it accepted that Chinese and Tamil could be taught as a third language. But Chinese and Indian schools were to remain outside the national system.[24]

In any event, the plan came to nothing because the federal treasury pointed out that there was not sufficient funds available to proceed on this basis. The position was summed up at the time in the following words:

> 'Though we unanimously affirm our belief, first that multiracial schools are essential for the education of the future citizens of a united Malayan nation; second, that there are two official languages, English and Malay, and both must be taught; and third, that there must be a

> single system of education and common content in the teaching in all schools, the country with its present level of expenditure, is not in a position to balance its annual budget'.[25]

This was not the end of the saga. Dato Abdul Razak bin Hussein, then Minister of Education, and later to become prime minister of Malaysia after the resignation of Tunku Abdul Rahman in 1970, headed a committee of experts in September 1955 to enquire into the state of education in the Federation, and prepared a report, many of the recommendations of which were enshrined in the 1957 Education Ordinance. Subsequently yet another committee was appointed under Abdul Rahman bin Talib, who succeeded Razak as Minister of Education, to examine the working of the Razak Report in the light of experience. The pivotal point of the new policy was contained in section 3 of the 1957 Education Ordinance, which reads as follows:

> 'The educational policy of the Federation is to enshrine a national system of education acceptable to the people as a whole which will satisfy their needs and promote their cultural, social, economic and political development as a nation, with the intention of making the Malay language the national language of the country whilst preserving and sustaining the growth of the language and culture of peoples other than Malays living in the country.'[26]

The question was how the new policy was to be translated into action, and the Talib Report (1960) dealt with this under the following headings: (1) the provision of primary education at government expense in each of the four main languages of Malaya, viz., Malay, English, Chinese and Tamil; (2) the bringing together of all the language streams at secondary level in fully assisted, national-type secondary schools using mainly either Malay or English as the medium of instruction; (3) the use of these two 'official' languages for both instruction and examination purposes; and (4) the establishment of common syllabi and timetables for all schools.

It should be borne in mind that by the time (we are rather anticipating our account) Malay had become the national language, English was permitted to be used until 1967 as an alternate official language. In other words, it was clear that after 1967 Malay would be the sole official language and the main medium of instruction in all fully assisted national-type secondary schools.

The Chinese reacted vigorously to this policy by demanding that Chinese should be recognized as an official language in the same way as Malay and English, and that public examinations should be held in Chinese. The cry that the government was killing the Chinese language was raised. The government replied by pointing out that under the new educational policy, Chinese (as a subject) could be learnt 'from the lowest to the highest rungs' of the educational ladder. Furthermore, it was stressed that primary education would be free for the first time in the history of Malaya, and a Chinese child could obtain six years of primary education wholly in the Chinese medium without paying fees. 'If we do not accept this education system,' the prime minister said, 'thousands of children passing out each year from the Chinese schools will not have the same opportunity as those who graduate from other schools, such as English schools. If they cannot get jobs because of their unacceptable qualifications, they will grow up hating the Government.'[27]

All Chinese schools were required to decide by the end of 1961 whether they would be either fully assisted (national-type secondary schools) using Malay or English as the main medium of instruction, or independent, in which case they could continue to use Chinese as the main medium of instruction, but would not receive any financial aid whatsoever from the government.

Some prominence has been given to the educational problems which have bedevilled Malaya because education was (and still is) a sensitive issue, and the discussions which they occasioned penetrated to the very heart of Sino-Malay friction, and highlighted the opposition by the Chinese to a policy which they interpreted as an attempt 'to deny their children the right to their own language and culture and turn them into pseudo-Malays ....'[28]

In the meantime, in early 1949, another attempt was made to bridge the gap between the Malays and the Chinese, and to bring about interracial harmony prior to the granting of self-government, as many people were concerned lest Malaya be destroyed by communal warfare such as that which had split India and Pakistan at the time of independence.[29]

As a result of the initiative of Malcolm MacDonald, the Commissioner-General for Southeast Asia, a Communities Liaison Committee (CLC) was established with Malay, Chinese, Indian, Eurasian and European community leaders on it. The CLC's aim was to find a way to eliminate interracial friction so as to create a united Malayan nation. The CLC proposed that all government and government-aided primary schools should teach Malay and English. It suggested that elections to local and federal councils should be introduced as soon as possible, and the citizenship requirements liberalized, to make it easier for non-Malays to acquire citizenship. The Chinese were called upon to be sympathetic towards and to help with the economic advancement of the Malays. In many ways, MacDonald, who was the committee's liaison officer, and Dato Onn and Tan Cheng Lock, who were the members of the CLC representing the Malay and Chinese communities, were idealists and ahead of their time, and the two community leaders found it difficult to carry their respective parties with them in their support of the CLC's proposals, which represented a non-communal approach in contrast to UMNO's and MCA's communal policies. UMNO and MCA were communal parties.[30]

In fact, when Dato Onn attempted to persuade UMNO to accept some of the CLC's proposals, he encountered stiff opposition from chauvinist Malay elements, or 'ultras', who supported the 'Malaya for the Malays' policy. The situation became even more strained when he recommended that the name of UMNO should be changed to United *Malayan* National Organization, which indicated that he was thinking along non-communal lines, and not long afterward, in mid-1951, he resigned from UMNO, and Tunku Abdul Rahman was elected President.[31]

Within a few weeks, Dato Onn had founded a new non-communal political party called the Independence of Malaya Party (IMP). Sir Henry Gurney, Malcolm MacDonald, and Tan Cheng Lock gave their encouragement and blessing to the new party, which fitted in with their concept of an interracial party. IMP announced a platform of economic and political equality, a common citizenship for all, the opening of the Malayan Civil Service (MCS) to Chinese and Indians, with the goal of independence within ten years.

But the tacit support and encouragement of the British may have been the kiss of death as many Malay nationalists regarded IMP as a British creation, and would not have anything to do with it.

Dato Onn had hoped that UMNO would cooperate with IMP but the fear of the Malays that his policy towards the Chinese was too lenient, and that Malay 'special rights' would be eroded, held them back. They were concerned, too, that independence within a decade would not allow them sufficient time to redress the economic balance between themselves and the Chinese.[32] Malay chauvinists within UMNO regarded Dato Onn as a traitor to the Malay cause.

The Federation of Malaya Agreement had included a promise of elections in due course, but due to the outbreak of the Emergency, the first municipal elections in Kuala Lumpur were not held until February 1952. It was thought that IMP had a good chance of winning a majority, but its hopes were shattered by the unexpected formation of an electoral alliance between the Selangor branches of the MCA and UMNO to contest the elections. The UMNO-MCA Alliance won nine of the twelve seats contested and inflicted a rousing defeat on IMP.

This successful *ad hoc* experiment, which had not been approved by the respective party national headquarters, was repeated at other municipal elections held in 1951 and 1952. In August 1953, it was decided to form a national Alliance, and in October 1954, the MIC joined, so that the Alliance came to represent a coalition of the major political parties of the three main racial groups in Malaya. UMNO-MCA-MIC still remained completely independent of each other, with their own organizations and structures, but at least it was possible for their national leaders to work out by discussion and compromise a common approach which enabled the Alliance to present a united front on most issues. Controversial matters were, as far as possible, not given a public airing.[33] Tan Cheng Lock was shrewd enough to realize that the way to working out a *modus vivendi* with the Malays lay through UMNO, with whose leaders he could hope to trade economic advantages for political power.

The first general elections were held in Malaya in 1955, and the Alliance swept to victory winning 51 out of 52 seats, although UMNO and the MCA were unable to reach accord on the question of citizenship and nationality rights for non-Malays. Tan Cheng Lock's stand was that the principle of *jus soli* should be adopted whereby citizenship would be automatically conferred on all persons born in Malaya, while the Malays jealously guarded their citizenship rights and wanted to retain the more restrictive citizenship provisions contained in the Federation of Malaya Agreement.[34]

In addition to the elected members of the Federal Legislative Council, there were 32 appointed members, but the Alliance was confident of counting on the support of 19 of them which gave it a majority of 70 in the Council of 98. Tunku Abdul Rahman became the first chief minister of the new government.[35]

UMNO was the leading partner in the UMNO-MCA-MIC Alliance as it carried more electoral weight than the non-Malay parties. 84 per cent of the 2,800,000 registered voters for the election were Malays, 11 per cent Chinese and approximately 5 per cent Indians. It has been estimated that there were about 600,000 Chinese eligible to vote but only 143,000 went to the polls. The Chinese were evidently still not very enthusiastic about becoming involved in public affairs.[36]

Tunku Abdul Rahman had said during the election campaign that if the Alliance were elected it would aim for self-government within two years and the establishment of an 'independent commission' to draw up a constitution for the attainment of independence within four. But the Tunku was pressed by the UMNO youth section to accelerate this time scale and work for independence within two years only.

Consequently, a Constitutional Conference was convened in London early in 1956, and attended by representatives of the Alliance, the Malay rulers and the British government.

The British government made it clear from the beginning that it was prepared to concede independence without a struggle, and the negotiations proceeded smoothly. It was agreed that independence within the British Commonwealth would be granted by 31 August 1957, if possible, which was the target date set by the Tunku, and that a Constitutional Commission, headed by Lord Reid, should be set up to draft a constitution. Its terms of reference included 'a common nationality for the whole of the Federation' and 'the safe-guarding of the special position of the Malays and the legitimate interests of other communities'.[37]

The commission met in Malaya from June to October 1956, and the most important views it considered were those presented to it by the Alliance Party, especially as the Alliance Party had such an overwhelming majority at both federal and state levels.

The leaders of the three communal parties making up the national Alliance agreed to speak with one voice to the commission and any differences which they might have had were resolved before their representations were put up to the commission. This is the origin of the 'bargain' or 'pact' between the UMNO and the MCA leaders whereby as a *quid pro quo* the MCA conceded that the 'special rights' of the Malays should be protected, in return for UMNO conceding that Chinese and other non-Malays should be granted 'easier' citizenship rights based on the principle of *jus soli,* as well as allowing the Chinese a free hand to pursue their business interests.[38]

However, the bargaining behind the scenes was intense at times and threatened to split the Alliance apart. Once again, the sensitive issue of citizenship rights, national language, education policy and the Malay special rights came up. While Tunku Abdul Rahman and Tan Cheng Lock were able to come to terms with each other because they were both western-educated liberals (the Tunku being a prince of the royal house of Kedah, who had been educated at Cambridge and had lived for many years in Britain, and Tan Cheng Lock a wealthy *baba* from Malacca, speaking English as his mother tongue, and knowing no Chinese, who was completely sincere in owning allegiance to no other country but Malaya), they had to contend with the extremists in both their parties. Neither the 'ultras' in UMNO nor the more chauvinistic Chinese-educated group in the MCA were willing to make concessions, and both factions at branch level began to pass resolutions demanding that the Merdeka (Independence) Constitution should contain provisions beneficial to their community.

Nevertheless, the Alliance leaders stood firm about not allowing any of the three communal parties to make separate submissions to the Reid Commission, and the day was saved.[39]

When the Reid Commission's draft proposals were published in 1957, objections were raised by both Malays and Chinese. The commission had accepted most of the points recommended by the Alliance but it had introduced certain ideas of its own, and it had accepted suggestions made by the Malay rulers and other interested parties. In general, the Malays were disappointed that their special rights had not been provided for, and the Chinese were dissatisfied with sections of the report relating to citizenship and the special status of the Chinese language which they felt did not go far enough.

The draft proposals were then reviewed and amended by a working committee in Malaya, and representatives of the Alliance, the Malay rulers, and the British government at a meeting in London. The new Merdeka Constitution for an independent Malaya emerged from these deliberations.[40]

The provisions of the Merdeka Constitution are worthy of analysis as they provide the framework of the Malaysia Constitution (1963) which was brought about by amending the Merdeka Constitution rather than redrafting a completely new constitution,[41] and they contain provisions covering the special rights and privileges of the Malays, national language, religion, and several other issues, which were (and still are) matters of contention between the Malays and Chinese.[42]

It was agreed to grant Malayan citizenship on the principle of *jus soli* to any person born in the Federation after 31st August 1957, as well as to make it easier for non-Malays to become citizens by registration and naturalization. This was an extremely controversial issue as the Malays were concerned lest it would eventually lead to their political primacy being challenged by the Chinese. It undoubtedly represented a major concession on the part of the Malays as it would increase the voting strength of the Chinese, and UMNO only agreed to it in exchange for the Chinese not objecting to other sections of the constitution which protected Malay special rights.[43]

The Reid proposals had provided for the continuation of the special rights and privileges for Malays, and these were covered by the constitution. They were in four main areas: Malay land reservations; the reserving of a quota of licences for certain businesses; the operation of a quota in the Malayan Civil Service whereby appointments would be in the ratio of one non-Malay to every four Malays; and special quotas for scholarships and educational grants.

In fact, this policy was a continuation of the policy enunciated by General Sir Gerald Templer (High Commissioner 1951—1954) in a speech to the Legislative Council in November 1952. 'Members of the Council,' he said, 'will, however, I feel sure agree that it is very necessary that the special position of the Malays should be retained in the Civil Service and imposed in the whole economic field. To this end, certain safeguards are necessary. I therefore propose that, as one of the safeguards, the number of non-Malay Federal citizens who are admitted into the Malayan Civil Service shall be limited to one for every four Malays admitted into that Service in the future. Other safeguards to secure and improve the position of the Malays are under consideration.'[44]

In regard to commerce and industry, Templer thought it

necessary that 'the Malays should be encouraged and assisted to play a full part in the economic life of the country so that the present uneven economic balance should be redressed'.[45]

The Reid Report proposed that the special position of the Malays should be reviewed after fifteen years with a view to their eventual withdrawal, but this suggestion was strongly opposed by UMNO, and not included in the constitution, which set no time limit.[46]

However, Malay privileges were augmented in the constitution in several ways. The states were allowed to retain or increase Malay land reservations until the area represented fifty per cent of the total area available for general private land use. Also, Penang and Malacca, not being Malay states, were given the right to institute Malay land reservations on the same terms as the nine Malay states making up the Federation. Under the constitution, land policy relating to Malay reservations was made more difficult to amend than the constitution itself. The constitution could only be amended by a two-thirds vote in the wholly-elected House of Representatives and the appointed Senate.

Bearing in mind the paramount political position of the Malays and the comparative strengths of the Malay and Chinese electorates consisting of federal citizens, the possibility of the constitution being amended to the detriment of the Malay community was very remote.

Under the constitution, Islam became the state religion although every person was allowed the right to practise his own religion. The sultans were the head of the Muslim religion in their own states and the Yang di-Pertuan Agong (the Paramount Ruler, a single, constitutional monarch elected for a term of five years by the Conference of Rulers) was responsible for the Muslim religion in Penang and Malacca.

Malay was made the national language but English was permitted to be used in parliament, the state legislatures and courts of law for a period of at least ten years from Merdeka Day (31 August 1957), until otherwise provided by parliament. No other language could be used in legislative proceedings, but federal and state governments had the right 'to preserve and sustain the use and study of the language of any community'.[47]

The consent of the Rulers Conference was required on matters dealing with the 'special position of the Malays or the legitimate interests of other communities', as well as the approval of the state governments and the federal government.

An important part of the 'pact' between UMNO and the MCA which was not explicitly referred to in the constitution was that the Chinese were allowed to continue to play a dominant role in the economic life of the country.[48]

After the ratification of the Merdeka Constitution, Malaya's independence was proclaimed, and at the stroke of midnight on 30 August 1957, the Union Jack was lowered at an impressive ceremony on the Selangor Club Padang in Kuala Lumpur, and the flag of the new independent Federation of Malaya hoisted in its place.[49]

Tunku Abdul Rahman campaigning in the 1955 elections.

Tunku Abdul Rahman (seated centre) and members of the Federation of Malaya Cabinet after swearing in at the Istana Negara, Kuala Lumpur, in August 1959. Dato Abdul Razak bin Hussein (Deputy Premier and Defence Minister) is seated second from left.

UMNO political meeting in Johore Bahru on 1 July 1954, with banners proclaiming *Merdeka* (Independence).

Malcolm MacDonald arrives in Malaya (1946) to take up his appointment as Governor-General Southeast Asia. Behind him, on the right, is Lord Louis Mountbatten, with Sir Ralph Hone, Chief Civil Affairs Officer for Malaya, in the rear.

Dato Harun bin Haji Idris, Menteri Besar, Selangor.

Lieutenant-General Sir Harold Briggs, Director of Operations.

Dato Onn bin Ja'afar hands over the leadership of UMNO in August 1951 to Tunku Abdul Rahman (at right).

Tan Siew Sin campaigning in the 1969 elections.

Syed Ja'afar Albar with a picket at the UMNO General Assembly, May 1965. The placard in Jawi reads *Ganyang Lee Kuan Yew* (Crush Lee Kuan Yew).

Sir Henry Gurney takes the oath of office as High Commissioner of the Federation of Malaya on 6 October 1948. On the right is Sir Alex New-boult, the Chief Secretary.

Tun Abdul Razak bin Dato Hussein, Prime Minister of Malaysia, arrives by helicopter to check on development progress.

Dato Sir Cheng-Lock Tan receiving the insignia of KBE from the Malaysian High Commissioner, General Sir Gerald Templer, on 5 June 1952.

Datuk Seri Dr. Mahathir Mohamad.

Lee Kuan Yew (August 1965) announcing the expulsion of Singapore from Malaysia.

Chapter Six

Prelude to the 13 May 1969 Riots

On 27 May 1961, Tunku Abdul Rahman, Prime Minister of the Federation of Malaya, was invited to address a lunch meeting of the Foreign Correspondents Association of Southeast Asia in Singapore. In his after-lunch speech, he proposed a 'Grand Malaysian Alliance' of Malaya, Singapore, Sarawak, British North Borneo and Brunei.

This was not the first time the idea had been proposed. It had been mooted by Malcolm MacDonald when he was British Commissioner-General for Southeast Asia (1949—1952). The first mention of such an amalgamation had been made by Lord Brassey in 1887, and in more recent times there had been several other organizations and persons who had advocated the same thing.[1]

There had been other proposals too. One of these concerned the linking up of Singapore and Malaya, on the grounds that both territories formed a single economic unit which had been divided artificially by the British.[2]

The problem, from the Malay point of view, was that the inclusion of Singapore's predominantly Chinese population would have affected the delicate racial balance, and there was a fear, too, that Singapore could easily move to the left.

Another proposal was a union between Malaya and the three Borneo territories of British North Borneo, Brunei and Sarawak. According to 'unimpeachable Chinese and Malay sources', the British had said to Kuala Lumpur 'you can't have Borneo without Singapore'.[3] This 'Greater Federation' concept attracted considerable UMNO support during the period from 1956 to 1960 as it appealed to Malay nationalists who thought of the indigenous peoples of Borneo as Malays,[4] and they saw it as strengthening their position *vis-a-vis* the Chinese.

By 1961, however, the Tunku was prepared to accept Singapore in Malaysia, as he had become convinced by Prime Minister Lee Kuan Yew of Singapore that the position of the ruling People's Action Party (PAP) was threatened by communist elements and that it would be more dangerous for Malaya to keep Singapore outside Malaysia than to take it inside. The Tunku himself said that for reasons of 'national security' and 'mutual economy' the two countries should work together. Moreover, by bringing in British Borneo, it was hoped that the indigenous peoples of Borneo, who outnumbered the Chinese there by three to one, would balance the Chinese majority in Singapore.[5]

Between May 1961 and September 1963 (when Malaysia came into existence), there was a series of consultations and negotiations[6], but when all was said and done, the real issue at stake was whether the Chinese and Malays could get on well together. It was apparent that the Malays still felt apprehensive of those Chinese 'who think and talk of everything Chinese and do not give any indication that they are Malayan in outlook'.[7] Tunku Abdul Rahman had also touched on the same point in his after-lunch speech referred to above when he had said that the tendency of the Chinese in Singapore was to try and make Singapore a 'little China' while in Malaya 'the Government is characteristically Malayan and bases its policy on a Malayan way of life and Malayan standards'.[8]

There were reservations in North Borneo and Sarawak, too, about Malaysia, the real reason being a genuine fear among the non-Muslim elements, who formed the majority of the population, that Malaysia would mean the imposition on them of Malay as the national language and Islam as the state religion, with Malay 'overlords' from Kuala Lumpur in place of British administrators.

In fact, this fear was unwarranted as, when the Malayan government amended the constitution by passing the Malaysia Act (1963), it allowed for both English and Malay to be used as official languages in North Borneo and Sarawak for a period of ten years, and even 1973 was not definitely set as a 'cut-off' date for the use of English. Moreover, Islam was not made the state religion of these two territories.[9]

Under the new Malaysian constitution, Singapore, too, was treated differently by being allowed to retain control of its education, labour and other matters. Singapore citizenship was accepted as being the equivalent of Federation of Malaya citizenship.

The new state of Malaysia incorporating the territories of Malaya, Singapore, Sarawak, and North Borneo (thereafter to be known as Sabah, its original Malay name), came into being on 16

September 1963. The Sultan of Brunei was initially disposed to join Malaysia but he subsequently changed his mind, most likely because he was not satisfied that the financial arrangements would be in Brunei's favour, especially as Brunei is an oil-rich state, and possibly, too, because his status vis-a-vis the Malay rulers of Peninsular Malaysia was not acceptable.

Singapore withdrew from Malaysia in mid-1965 but this will be touched upon later in this account.

It had originally been intended by Tunku Abdul Rahman that the birth of the new state would date from 31 August 1963 but its inception was delayed until the following month by objections from Indonesia and the Philippines.[10]

Malaysia from the beginning was a plural society, but there was no sign of integration among the various races living in it. In its place, as far as the Malays and Chinese were concerned, there was a rather precarious agreement or understanding between the UMNO and the MCA top leaders that Malay special rights should not be questioned and the political predominance of the Malays should not be challenged provided that the Chinese were allowed to pursue unimpeded their traditional commercial and industrial activities.

There was a certain ambivalence and inexactness about the latter part of the 'pact', as it was, at the same time, accepted that the Malays should use their political predominance to improve their economic position to redress the economic balance between the two communities so that they could play a more significant part in the economic life of the country. It seemed inevitable that there would be some intrusion on what the Chinese regarded as their preserve even though the reshaping of the economic balance, and the adjusting of the scales, was to be done without depriving anyone of what they already had.

When General Templer was appointed High Commissioner of the Federation of Malaya in February 1952, he had been issued with a directive by the British government that the 'ideal of a united Malayan nation does not involve the sacrifice by any community of its traditional culture and customs, but before it can be fully realized the Malays must be encouraged and assisted to play a full part in the economic life of the country, so that the present uneven economic balance may be redressed'.[11]

As a result of this policy, various quasi-government bodies and institutions came into existence, such as the Federal Land

Development Authority (FELDA) in 1956. This large organization was engaged in land development and settlement projects, with the objects of improving the standard of living and increasing the income of the rural population, which was mainly made up of Malay peasants, and opening up new land for high yield rubber and oil palm for Malay settlers.[12]

Another body worthy of note was the Rural and Industrial Development Authority (RIDA) established in 1950, which was reorganized fifteen years later into the Majlis Amanah Ra'ayat (Council of Trust for the Indigenous People) (MARA). Affiliated to this body was the MARA Institute of Technology which started in an unpretentious way in 1954 as a coir and rope-making centre and was expanded into a full-scale Institute for Business and Professional Studies in 1960.

During 1966–70, MARA made available about 4,800 loans totalling M$31 million for various projects, mainly to Malay businessmen and proto-industrialists. It established a number of companies in the field of commerce and industry for producing such items as *batik* garments, tapioca starch, rubber pellets and processed rubber. It built shophouses for Malay businessmen, and encouraged *bumiputras* (see below) to go into business as wholesale suppliers and contractors for construction materials.

MARA also formed and operated bus companies (most of the transport companies in Malaysia were run by Chinese), and by 1970 it was operating 360 buses and providing services covering 2,000 miles. By this time, and after setting the transport companies on their feet, MARA had transferred six of its bus services to Malay concerns leaving 33 still under its own direct operational control.[13]

Other organizations included the Federal Agricultural Marketing Authority (FAMA), established in 1952, to improve the marketing system and to ensure that farmers obtained a fair price for their products, and the Bank Bumiputra, which was formed in 1965. 'Bumiputra', meaning literally 'princes of the soil' but usually translated more prosaically as 'sons of the soil', was the name used for what were referred to in the constitution as Malays and other indigenous people.

The Bank Pertanian Malaysia (Agricultural Bank), set up in 1969, was used by the Malaysian government for making agricultural credit available to Malay farmers on reasonable terms, and the funds for this purpose were channelled through rural cooperatives and Farmers' Associations.

The setting up of more effective machinery for extending and coordinating credit facilities to Malay farmers was intended to break the effective control which Chinese and Indian (*chettiar*) money lenders and entrepreneurs had over agricultural land belonging to Malays. This was done by advancing money to the Malay farmers for which collateral was provided by pledging the land as security. In fact, as has been mentioned earlier, an attempt had already been made in 1933 to deal with this problem by the passing of the Malay Reservation Enactment in the FMS and similar laws in the UMS which forbade charge or lease of Malay Reservation land to a non-Malay.

But this measure was not entirely effective in reducing Malay indebtedness to non-Malays, as shopkeepers and rice-millers, who were for the most part Chinese, devised a system referred to as *padi kunca* whereby a farmer could obtain a loan or credit facilities against the security of *padi* not yet harvested. Under this ingenious system of 'forward credit', instead of the land being pledged as a security for cash, as this was now forbidden, the produce of the land was pledged instead. To give a practical example, a Malay scholar working in this field in the late 1960s relates the case of a rice-mill and two shops in Kangkong granting Malay farmers credit of from M$40 to M$50 during the off-season against their future crop of *padi,* which was to be repaid with a quantum of padi bearing a market value of around M$80. Thus the resulting profit to the Chinese entrepreneurs would be between 60 to 100 per cent.[14]

There was a similar system to *padi kunca* in the fresh fish trade where Chinese middlemen commonly advanced rice and cloth, and sometimes money, to Malay fishermen during the off-season in anticipation of being able to purchase their catch during the fishing season at an agreed price depressed below market level.[15]

Under the *First Malaysia Plan 1966—70,* more secondary schools were built in rural areas, and residential facilities were provided in some urban secondary schools, so that Malay pupils from the rural areas, particularly in science streams, could board at them. As a result of these programmes, more than three-quarters of the primary schools and about one half of the secondary schools were located in rural areas. This was a great help to the *bumiputras* who had been at a disadvantage previously as the secondary schools were mainly in the towns whereas most of the Malays were rural dwellers.[16]

The period of the *First Malaysia Plan* was characterized by a high rate of development activity in the country. The long MCP-inspired Emergency had come to an end in 1960, and the government was able to concentrate more on development projects rather than security. The private sector of the economy sprang to life again with renewed vigour to take advantage of the opportunities for growth investment. A new Ministry of National and Rural Development was formed to ensure the speedy and efficient implementation of the rural development programme. The emphasis was placed on rural rather than urban development and progress, which benefited the Malays more than anyone else. In fact, the Malays made up only 28 per cent of the total urban population of Peninsular Malaysia in 1970, with the Chinese accounting for 58 per cent and the Indians 13 per cent.[17]

In describing the decade between 1960—1970, the *Second Malaysia Plan* says: 'Despite the significant progress made in improving the economic well-being of the have-nots, the problem of economic imbalance remained. Although there were some movements out of agriculture as well as into more productive activities within the agricultural sector, a large part of the population continued to be engaged in low-income activities in the rural areas. Indications are that wide gaps in income and living conditions between the traditional sector (both rural and urban) and the modern sector continued to exist. They arose from differing opportunities for education, employment and ownership of or access to entrepreneurial resources. These differences were accentuated by the concentration of Malays and other indigenous people in the low-income activities.'[18]

It is evident from this statement which way the government was thinking, and accordingly when the *Second Malaysia Plan 1971—75* was drafted, it dealt with these imbalances and differences, particularly those between the Malay and Chinese communities.

There is an interesting section in the *Second Malaysia Plan* dealing with the decade leading up to 1970, which is well worth close study as it demonstrates very clearly the Malay perception that they were in danger of 'losing out' to the non-Malays in regard to the ownership of the Malaysian economy in terms of the pattern of ownership, distribution of wealth, and participation in the modernization and developmental process.[19] There was clearly a genuine fear that economically, at any rate, the Malays had been left behind by the non-Malays, and that unless something was done about it before it was too late, they would be 'overwhelmed' in their own country.

Most of the development was seen to be taking place in the urban areas and not in the rural areas, where the Malays lived in their *kampungs*. As has been brought out above, the majority of the inhabitants of the towns were non-Malay. The concentration of Chinese in the three major towns of Peninsular Malaysia, that is, Kuala Lumpur (the federal capital), Penang and Ipoh, was indeed very striking. Outwardly, with the ethnic composition of the inhabitants, and their colourful Chinese shop signs, they gave the appearance of being Chinese settlements, with little sign at all of Malay influence. In 1970, about 41 per cent of the urban Chinese and 19 per cent of all the Chinese in Peninsular Malaysia lived in these three towns.[20]

As the quality of life, as well as social amenities and economic opportunities seemed to be better in urban areas than rural areas, and the majority of urban dwellers were Chinese, while the Malays lived in the rural areas, the economic imbalance could be interpreted in racial terms. Thus, the major concentration of Malays was in the traditional rural sector of the economy, which consisted of subsistence agriculture, including single-crop *padi,* the gathering of jungle produce, inshore fishing, and so on, while, on the other hand, the modern urban sector of the economy comprised technically advanced industry and the modern services, including the professions and the tourist trade, was dominated by non-Malay and foreign companies.

In the late 1960s, hardly any rubber estates of 100 acres and above in Peninsular Malaysia were owned by Malays, although Malays and non-Malays shared ownership of rubber smallholdings. The ownership of the rubber, oil palm, and coconut industries was in the hands of non-Malays, even taking into account about 308,000 acres of FLDA (now FELDA) land cultivated with rubber and oil palm which had been settled predominantly by Malays.[21]

In 1969, the Malays had only 1.0 per cent share of the share capital of resident limited companies in Peninsular Malaysia, although the Chinese had 22.8 per cent, and foreign controlled companies or branches of companies incorporated overseas had the largest share of all.

The above facts will speak for themselves, and, as a result, the government set a target that within twenty years at least 30 per cent of the management and ownership of all commercial and industrial activities should be in the hands of the *bumiputras*.[22] It was the first time in the history of Malaya that such a major readjustment and restructuring of the economy had been proposed, and the ripples of this policy inevitably increased the tension between the Malays and the Chinese.

It will be remembered that Singapore's entry into Malaysia was not without its difficulties and that the Malays in Peninsular Malaysia were always rather wary about Singapore's 'Chineseness'. The Chinese in Singapore made up 75 per cent of the total population. From the Malay point of view the ruling People's Action Party (PAP) in Singapore was a Chinese party with a Chinese leader, and not a noncommunal party, even though it had non-Chinese members.[23] Smooth and harmonious relations between Singapore and Kuala Lumpur, the Malaysian capital, depended on each side being aware of the fragile nature of the *modus vivendi* between the two main communities, and taking care not to tread on each other's toes. This was not to be, however. The attitudes and styles of the PAP in Singapore and the Alliance in Malaysia were poles apart. The PAP had a brash, aggressive image, and it was accustomed to winning points by debate in which no punches were pulled while UMNO was much more conservative and deliberate, and it was used to settling disputes by mutual agreement before making any public announcement.

The decision on the part of the PAP to take a 'token part' in the April 1964 federal elections in Peninsular Malaysia came as a surprise, as Lee Kuan Yew had given an undertaking to Tunku Abdul Rahman that the PAP had no such intention.[24] The PAP made it clear that it wanted to replace the MCA as UMNO's Chinese partner in the UMNO-MCA-MIC Alliance, but Tunku Abdul Rahman announced that he would stand by the MCA and he would not jettison it for the PAP.[25]

This blunted the thrust of the PAP, and although it was careful in the election campaign to focus its attack on the MCA, and indeed praise Tunku Abdul Rahman and UMNO, in the eyes of UMNO, the PAP's move into the Malaysian political arena was seen as a challenge to their own political supremacy.[26]

The results of the federal election proved that the PAP had made a serious tactical error in entering the field. Only one of the nine PAP candidates was elected, and even he only obtained a majority of 808 votes.[27] The Alliance captured 89 of the 104 federal parliamentary seats. The MCA won 27 of these seats out of the 34 it contested, which was a clear victory for them over the PAP. In the elections for the state assemblies, which were held simultaneously with the federal elections, the Alliance won 241 seats and the PAP none.[28]

After its electoral defeat in Peninsular Malaysia, the PAP decided to stay in politics in Malaysia as part of the opposition and Lee Kuan Yew formed a new coalition of opposition parties called the Malaysia Solidarity Consultative Convention with the slogan of 'Malaysian Malaysia'. Significantly, the group's manifesto maintained that 'the nation and state is *(sic)* not identified with the supremacy, well-being and interest of any one community or race'.[29]

This confirmed the suspicions of some of the UMNO 'ultras' that the PAP itself was against everything that UMNO stood for, and that it was not disposed to accept the special rights and position of the Malays, although Lee Kuan Yew was to say in April 1965 that the PAP upheld Malay privileges in the constitution. However, he added that these privileges would help only 'a small group of Malay bourgeoisie to become capitalists', and would not be of much assistance to the Malay *ra'ayat* (peasants).[30]

While the PAP was intent on establishing itself in Peninsular Malaysia, UMNO and the MCA had their own plans for gaining a foothold in Singapore.[31] The MCA attempt came to naught but UMNO's incursion brought serious results in its train. It was headed by Syed Ja'afar Albar, Secretary-General of UMNO, who was called an 'ultra' by Lee Kuan Yew.

Albar had made several inflammatory speeches in Singapore, and the *Utusan Melayu,* a Malay language newspaper printed in *Jawi* (Arabic) script, did not make matters any better by the anti-PAP and anti-Chinese tone of its editorials and news reports.[32] Matters came to a head in July 1964 when Sino-Malay riots broke out in the streets of Singapore on the occasion of a Muslim procession celebrating Prophet Muhammad's birthday. On the day before the riots, leaflets had appeared urging Malays to start a *jihad* (holy war) against the Chinese and slaughter them wherever they could be found.[33]

Singapore was placed under curfew. Police riot squads were brought in to quell the disturbances and although troops were called out in aid of the civil power, twenty-two people were killed and about five hundred injured before the disturbances could be brought under control.[34]

Tunku Abdul Rahman blamed the riots on Indonesian subversive elements (this was the time of Indonesian confrontation with Malaysia), who had aggravated the legitimate grievances of the Singapore Malays.[35]

In September 1964, there were again racial riots in Singapore, which coincided with the landing of Indonesian paratroops in the southern part of Peninsular Malaysia.[36] On this occasion, it was difficult to attribute the cause to any agitation by local, rather than foreign, elements of racial sentiments, and the Tunku again pointed out how easy it would be for Indonesian troublemakers to exploit the neglect of the Singapore Malay community by the Singapore government which 'made no provision for special treatment of one particular race or community'.[37]

The British colonial government in Singapore had claimed in 1949: 'There are no social problems of race or cultural relations of any magnitude. All races live and work harmoniously together.'[38] But though this may have been true, at least outwardly, while the British were in control, once independence came there was no 'umpire' to maintain the intercommunal balance, and interracial ill feeling came very close to the surface.

By May 1965, there was little doubt that Sino-Malay relations had become badly strained, and the Malays realized that they were no longer in the majority in Malaysia as they had been previously in the Federation of Malaya. Lee Kuan Yew had reached the point of openly challenging the special rights of the Malays. 'According to history,' he said, 'Malays began to migrate to Malaysia in noticeable numbers only about 700 years ago. Of the 39 per cent Malays in Malaysia today, about one-third of them are comparatively new immigrants like the secretary-general of UMNO, Dato Syed Ja'afar Albar, who came to Malaya from Indonesia just before the war at the age of more than thirty. Therefore it is wrong and illogical for a particular racial group to think that they are more justified to be called Malaysians and that the others can become Malaysian only through their favour.'

Lee Kuan Yew's statement was refuted by UMNO. Dato Abdul Razak, Deputy Prime Minister of Malaysia, said that 'Mr Lee has not only upset the Malays, but also the Rulers and everybody else ...If there is racial trouble, all of us, including Mr Lee, will suffer.'[39]

Lee Kuan Yew answered that he could trace his ancestry back one hundred years in Singapore, and again refuted the idea that the Malays were the indigenous people of the Malay archipelago, but he was careful to add that he supported the Malaysian constitution and Malay special rights.[40]

It was well that he did this because there was some talk at the time of the Malaysian government detaining him. It soon became evident that the situation was deteriorating fast, and relations between Singapore and the central government were rapidly approaching breaking point.

Tunku Abdul Rahman, the Malaysian Prime Minister, has put his views on record as follows: 'When facing this dilemma, I found that only two choices lay before me. One, take positive action against Mr Lee Kuan Yew; and, two, break with Singapore and save the nation from a bloodbath. So I chose the second course.'[41]

On 9 August 1965, the Tunku made an official announcement in the Dewan Rakyat (House of Commons) that Singapore would have to leave Malaysia.[42]

There is little doubt that Malaysia came dangerously close to racial violence at the time of Singapore's expulsion, and if matters had been allowed to drag on, it would have led to fighting between the Malays and Chinese on an unprecedented scale. A year later, the Tunku added the following afterthought: 'If we had not separated there would have been blue murder.'[43]

Even after the expulsion of Singapore from Malaysia, the PAP continued to concern itself with the position of the Chinese in Peninsular Malaysia, and the central government decided that the PAP branch in Malaysia would have to be wound up since it had become a 'foreign party'. In March 1966, the solitary PAP member of the Dewan Rakyat registered a 'new' party called the Democratic Action Party (DAP), which, while having a separate legal identity from the PAP, was clearly its successor in Peninsular Malaysia. It was a champion of the Malaysian Malaysia concept as presented by Lee Kuan Yew.[44]

In drawing this chapter in the history of 'Singapore in Malaysia' to a close, it should be noted that there were, in addition to the 'Malay vs. Chinese' undertones inherent in the situation, constitutional grounds for friction between the two governments relating to economic and financial issues. The differences between the two governments were exacerbated by such matters as whether Singapore would be allowed to develop as the main industrial centre of Malaysia, as well as the commercial centre, or whether Peninsular Malaysia's industry should be built up instead; the financial contribution Singapore was expected to make to the central government; and the loan Singapore was to make to East Malaysia, but these problems could no doubt have been resolved amicably by negotiation had it been possible for Singapore and Kuala Lumpur to build up mutual trust and respect, and enter into a dialogue.[45]

It will be recollected that the original provision about language in the constitution was that only Malay as the sole national and official language could be used in parliament and state legislatures after 1967, that is, ten years after Merdeka, unless otherwise provided by parliament.[46]

With the approach of 1967, the pressure for the wider use of Malay increased from the Dewan Bahasa dan Pustaka (Malaysia's Language and Literature Bureau), UMNO 'ultras' and other Malay nationalists. There was just as resolute counter-pressure from Chinese chauvinists in the MCA, other non-Malay political parties, and Chinese teachers.[47]

The Alliance took the formal and legal step required to create Malay as the sole national and official language by passing the National Language Act in 1967. However, while the position of Malay was affirmed, to the great and bitter disappointment of the Malay language advocates, English was still permitted to be used for some official purposes as deemed fit by the federal and state authorities, or by the Yang di-Pertuan Agong (Paramount Ruler).[48]

Tunku Abdul Rahman called for an all-out effort to promote the use of Malay, under the slogan *Bahasa Jiwa Bangsa* (Language is the Soul of the Nation) which was diplayed on posters, banners, and road signs all over the country. At the same time, he made it clear that he felt that English would have to be used as the language of higher studies for a long time to come.[49]

The outcome was that, on the one hand, non-Malays were decidedly unenthusiastic about the government's stand on language, especially as it was realized that the planned unification of the school system would lead to Malay becoming the sole medium of instruction, yet on the other hand, the Tunku and other top UMNO leaders were criticized severely by the Malay 'ultras' and their supporters, especially Malay schoolteachers and university students, for conceding too much to the Chinese.[50]

Chapter Seven

The 13 May Riots

During the long five-week election campaign leading up to the 1969 federal and state elections, it became apparent that the Alliance leaders were not in touch with the considerable sense of frustration and antagonism which had built up inexorably over the course of the past few years among non-Malays over such controversial issues as Malay special rights, the privileged position the Malays had in regard to employment, the four-to-one preponderance Malays enjoyed in the senior ranks of the civil service, and the barely concealed efforts that were being made to counter Chinese hegemony in commerce and industry. It has been said that 'The Chinese and Indians resident in Kuala Lumpur had after fifteen years of Alliance rule developed an acute persecution complex'.[1] Interracial friction seemed almost inevitable as a result of the racial insults which were bandied about indiscriminately and irresponsibly both by the opposition parties and the Alliance.

According to one observer, 'The unwritten law regarding communal issues was violated by both the Alliance and Opposition parties when they indulged in open public and heated debate over such subjects.'[2] Malay and Chinese emotions were rubbed raw and came dangerously close to breaking point. Although the campaign went off without incident, there was a distinct feeling of tension as polling day (10 May) approached.[3]

The Alliance leadership did not have any new formula for fighting the elections and countering the threat posed by the opposition parties consisting, in particular, of the Pan Malaysian Islamic Party (PMIP), the Democratic Action Party (DAP), the Gerakan Rakyat Malaysia (Gerakan), and the People's Progressive Party (PPP). The Alliance election manifesto read very much like a government report, and while it was a solid, reasoned document, it did not have any elan about it. It gave a summary of what the Alliance had achieved during its years in power, with sections devoted to the 'economic approach', 'defence and security', 'foreign affairs', and the 'racial nemesis'.

In regard to Sino-Malay relations, the most interesting section was the last-named. 'Historical circumstances have combined to keep the races apart', it said, 'and have somewhat segregated them economically.' The rural people are predominantly Malays, who are living at subsistence level and 'because we have given them a deserving priority in our attentions, we have been accused by our adversaries of practising racial discrimination'. It confirmed that the position of the 'have-nots' (the Malays) would have to be levelled up to the economic status of the 'haves' (the Chinese) although it added that this policy did not aim at depriving anyone of opportunities for advancement. It claimed that there was not a single opposition party which had shown itself capable of serving the needs of Malaysia's multiracial society, and the alternative to Alliance rule would be 'an irreversible process of disintegration with all the consequential carnage too hideous for anyone to envisage'.[4]

The Alliance placed considerable emphasis on maintaining Malay 'special rights' during the election campaign, and in a broadcast over Radio Malaysia on 9 May, the Tunku elucidated once again the division of power between the Malays and the Chinese. 'The Malays have gained for themselves political power,' he said. 'The Chinese and Indians have won for themselves economic power. The blending of the two with complete goodwill and understanding has brought about peace and harmony, coupled with prosperity to the country'.[5]

The main enemy as far as UMNO was concerned was the PMIP, which, as the oldest opposition party, had built up for itself a reputation as an Islamic religious and communal Malay party, with a strong anti-Chinese streak about it.

It promised that if it came to power it would establish an Islamic state in Malaysia, and amend the constitution to give it a more Malay rather than Malaysian slant. Its stand was crystallized in its slogan: *bangsa* (race), *ugama* (religion) and *tanah Melayu* (land of the Malays). The focal point of its power was Kelantan, but it had a not inconsiderable following in the Malay states of Trengganu, Perlis, Kedah as well as in north Penang, where the Malays formed a majority.

It accused UMNO of being pro-Chinese and selling out the country and the Malays to the Chinese.[6]

Its influence was not very strong in the west coast states where there were more non-Malays, and a greater degree of exposure to western-style modernization and economic development.[7]

UMNO countered this by alleging that the PMIP had links with the outlawed Malayan Communist Party (MCP) in south Thailand, which was a subtle thrust, as it will be remembered that the MCP was predominantly Chinese in its make-up. It pointed out that the PMIP had done nothing about the economic development of Kelantan although it had been in control of the state government there since 1959. UMNO offered tremendous sums of developmental aid to Kelantan (which were termed 'daylight political bribery' by the PMIP President) if the vote in the state election should swing in its favour.[8] Two further charges were made against the PMIP in order to discredit it in Malay eyes. Firstly, it was alleged that it had some sort of electoral understanding with the DAP, theoretically a noncommunal party, but which was regarded in Malay eyes as a Chinese party, with links extending south to the PAP in Singapore. Secondly, the Tunku claimed that it was receiving funds from the PAP in Singapore through the DAP.

This charge was taken so seriously by the Singapore government that it was officially denied by the Singapore Foreign Minister.

The PMIP and DAP then countercharged that the Alliance had received funds from the CIA, which the Tunku promptly denied by taking an oath on the Koran in a mosque.

The DAP was seen as posing the biggest threat to the MCA. Despite claims to be noncommunal, it was controlled by Chinese, and it attacked the MCA for surrendering Chinese rights to UMNO in the Alliance. Its platform was based on its 'Setapak Declaration of Principles', which was proclaimed by the General Executive Committee, together with members of branch committees, at Setapak near Kuala Lumpur on 29 July 1967. In brief, it was opposed to racial hegemony and supported the PAP's 'Malaysian Malaysia' concept. It saw Malaysia evolving as a multiracial, multilingual and multireligious society.[9] Its election manifesto was 'Towards a Malaysian Malaysia'. It was attacked by the Alliance as being an anti-Malay communal party opposed to Malay 'special rights' and as a cover organization for the PAP, the branches of which had been de-registered in Peninsular Malaysia after Singapore's departure from Malaysia.[10]

The DAP entered into an electoral pact with Gerakan and PPP aimed at preventing a split in opposition votes, and this strategy was to play an important part in the resounding blow given to the Alliance in the elections, which will be commented on later.[11]

The Gerakan was founded in 1968 as a noncommunal party by several leading intellectuals, as well as politicians who joined from the United Democratic Party (UDP), which was dissolved in 1968 in favour of the newly-established Gerakan, and others who crossed over from the Labour Party of Malaya (LPM).[12]

It is interesting to note that the UDP was formed in 1962 by Dr Lim Chong Eu, a medical practitioner and a former MCA President, who helped to sponsor Gerakan, and later became the chief minister of Penang.[13]

The LPM had a chequered history. It had been founded in the early 1950s, when its leaders were English-educated professional men, who were intellectual socialists, but they had left the party after it was infiltrated in the late 1950s by a large number of Chinese-educated Chinese. The latter were Chinese chauvinists from the 'non-Malay' states of Johore, Malacca, Selangor and Penang, who were virulently anti-Malay and strongly in favour of Chinese education and Chinese culture. The LPM was alleged by the government to have communist connections and to be an MCP-front organization.

The LPM took no part in the elections, most probably as a result of a policy decision taken by the MCP that the elections were a charade and should be boycotted.[14] Meanwhile, it had been involved in the murder of an UMNO member in Penang in April, just a fortnight before polling day, and ten days later, one of its members had been shot dead by the police while resisting arrest in Kuala Lumpur. The LPM held a large funeral procession in Kuala Lumpur on 9 May, one day before the elections, when serious communal violence was only narrowly averted by the good sense and patience of the police.[15]

According to an official report, the LPM 'defied Police instruction and organised a large parade in which an estimated number of ten thousand persons took part and marched through the centre of Kuala Lumpur, flouting every Police instruction. They chanted Maoist slogans, sang "The East is Red", and displayed portraits of Mao Tse-tung and the Red flag. The parade passed through the heart of Kuala Lumpur and tied up traffic in almost every major street in the city, and provoked Malay bystanders with shouts of *"Malai si!"* (Death to the Malays!) and *"Hutang darah dibayar darah!"* (Blood debts will be repaid with blood!)'.[16]

To revert to the Gerakan, its leading sponsors included Professor Syed Hussein Alatas, Professor of Malay Studies, University of Singapore, a Dutch-educated Malay intellectual from Johore, who became the party chairman; Professor Wang Gungwu, then Professor of History, University of Malaya; Dr. Lim Chong Eu; and Dr. Tan Chee Khoon, a former leader of LPM.

The Gerakan campaigned under the slogan of 'Equality, Justice and Equal Opportunities for All: Our Aim'.[17]

Among its aims were the reduction of the Alliance's two-third majority in parliament so that it would not 'further abrogate our constitutional rights and guarantees'. It was opposed to corruption which then posed a serious problem in Malaysia — Professor Alatas, in fact, wrote a book on this.[18]

While accepting the status and policy of Malay as the national language as provided for in the constitution, it was in favour of the 'legitimate use of all languages', and pressed for the support of the National and Merdeka Universities where Malay, Chinese and Tamil could be studied up to university level, and advocated the retention of Chinese and Tamil secondary education. It advocated an integrated Malaysian society with a common outlook and destiny.[19]

The sphere of influence of the People's Progressive Party (PPP) was Perak, where it had established itself as the champion of Chinese rights, under the leadership of two Ceylonese-Tamil lawyer brothers, one of whom died before the 1969 elections. Its election slogan was 'Malaysia for the Malaysians'. During the first federal elections of 1955, it had supported Malay special rights and the Alliance's position on the language and education issues. However, after independence, it had made a complete *volte face* by reshaping its policy to oppose Malay special rights, and had declared itself to be in favour of multilingualism and official recognition of the Chinese and Tamil languages. It had an even more pronounced pro-Chinese image than the DAP, and most of its supporters were Chinese, in spite of its president being a non-Chinese.[20]

Polling took place on 10 May. The results were received with dismay by the Alliance. Although at parliamentary level, the Alliance won 66 seats (see Appendix 4), and as ten of its candidates had been returned unopposed in Sabah, it was certain of a majority in the 144-strong Dewan Rakyat, the outcome of the elections in East Malaysia, which were staggered and not held at the same time as those in Peninsular Malaysia, would decide whether it would still retain a two-third majority in parliament, without which it would be powerless to amend the constitution unless it could enlist the support of some members of the opposition.[21]

The results meant that the Alliance had won 23 seats less than it had in the 1964 general elections or, in other words, it had lost 25.84 percent of the seats which it had formerly held.

The MCA position was affected most seriously of all. It had won only 13 of the 33 seats it contested, that is, 14 less than in 1964. The MCA's 14 losses were matched by 13 DAP gains. Moreover, of these 13 seats, three had been unopposed, and three were won in Malay-majority constituencies.

The MIC had won two out of the three seats it had contested. In 1964, it had won three.

UMNO, *primus inter pares* of the three parties making up the Alliance, had won 51 out of the 67 seats it had contested or, in other words, 8 less than in 1964.[22]

The Alliance, in the words of the *Straits Times,* had a 'rough time to victory'.[23]

The most dramatic shift away from the Alliance occurred in the state elections, which in Malaysia are held at the same time as the federal elections (see Appendix 5).[24]

Penang was lost to the Gerakan, where only 4 of UMNO's 24 candidates were returned, with Gerakan winning 16 seats, DAP 3, and another opposition party 1. Kelantan was held by the PMIP to the chagrin of UMNO which had planned to inflict a resounding defeat on its rival. The Gerakan and the DAP had considerable success in Selangor at the expense of the Alliance, which was particularly galling considering that Kuala Lumpur was not only the Selangor state capital but also the federal capital. In Selangor, the opposition won one half of the 28 seats (DAP 9, Gerakan 4, Independent 1), and in Perak, the Alliance was struggling to retain control. It had won only 19 out of the 40 state seats (PPP 12, DAP 6, Gerakan 2, PMIP 1).

It was fortunate for the Alliance that the Gerakan refused to join any coalition of opposition parties, so that the Alliance was able to hang on to the control of the Selangor and Perak legislatures.[25]

The situation was seen by the Malays to be extremely serious. An agonizing reappraisal of their position was called for. It was clear that the opposition parties had made a considerable dent in their armour, and the Alliance faced the prospect of a strong Chinese-based opposition in parliament for the first time since it had come to power.

UMNO campaign directors met behind closed doors as soon as possible after the results were known and demanded a more Malay-oriented Cabinet. It was urged that Malay ministers should be appointed to take over the portfolios of Commerce and Industry and Finance which had in the past always been held by Chinese ministers appointed from within the ranks of the MCA.[26] The Tunku's own standing in UMNO had fallen considerably after the passing of the National Language Act, when Malay national language advocates had criticized him for not taking a strong enough stand with the Chinese.

Although, technically speaking, the Alliance had won, the opposition parties were elated at the improvement of their position, and on 11 and 12 May the DAP and Gerakan held 'victory' parades in Kuala Lumpur, some of which did not have police permission, which were followed by numerous smaller processions.

Some of the DAP and Gerakan supporters went to the house of Dato Harun bin Idris, Menteri Besar (Chief Minister) of Selangor, and chairman of UMNO Selangor Branch, and told him to quit as he was no longer Menteri Besar.

The 'victory procession', writes Tunku Abdul Rahman, 'was held on an unprecedented scale, politically speaking, and was accompanied by acts of rowdyism and hooliganism and in utter defiance of the Police after the main procession had ended. The procession went through unauthorised routes, jamming traffic everywhere as a consequence...'[27]

This unruly mob slowly wound its way through town, past Kampung Bharu, the largest Malay residential area in Kuala Lumpur, where some thirty thousand Malays lived, hurling abuse and insults as it went, such as *'Melayu sudah jatuh'* (The Malays have fallen), *'Kuala Lumpur sekarang China punya'* (Kuala Lumpur now belongs to the Chinese), *'Ini negeri bukan Melayu punya, kita mahu halau semua Melayu'* (This country does not belong to the Malays, we want to chase out all the Malays), and the like.[28]

On the evening of 13 May, a group of UMNO supporters assembled outside the house of the Selangor Menteri Besar with the intention of staging a counter-demonstration on behalf of UMNO, and immediately after this procession got under way disturbances involving Malays and Chinese broke out.

Very soon after that, rioting occurred in several parts of Kuala Lumpur and it was clear that the government had a very serious emergency on its hands. Malays and Chinese indulged in an orgy of killing, looting and burning. The police did their best to control the situation in an even-handed way, but as the rioting continued to get out of hand, the army had to be called in, and police and army reinforcements were summoned from outside. The situation by then had become increasingly uncontrollable, and a curfew was declared at 8.00 p.m. on 13 May.

'Kuala Lumpur was a city on fire,' Tunku Abdul Rahman wrote in his account of the disturbances. 'I could clearly see the conflagration from my residence at the top of the hill and it was a sight that I never thought I would see in my lifetime. In fact all my work to make Malaysia a happy and peaceful country through these years, and also my dream of being the happiest Prime Minister in the world, were also going up in flames.'[29]

On 14 May, intermittent shooting occurred in different parts of the town, and roving gangs of Malays and Chinese, several hundred strong, fought savagely with each other using any weapons they could lay their hands on. As the London *Times* correspondent reported, 'in street after street were overturned and burnt-out cars, motor-cycles and scooters, with no evidence of the fate that befell their passengers'.

The bloodshed continued on 15 May, and there was firing between the army and armed youths. Clouds of dense black smoke continued to rise from burning houses, shops and markets, and the roads were littered with debris and barricades.

It is not necessary to recount here blow-by-blow the bitter fighting which took place between the two main communities of Malaysia, and the havoc and destruction to life and property that was wrought, but rioting, arson and looting continued for several days before the situation was brought under control.[30] A 24-hour curfew was imposed over virtually the whole of the west coast of Peninsular Malaysia, that is, Selangor, Negri Sembilan, Perak, Kedah, Penang, and Malacca. During the height of the flare-up, rail, bus, train and air links with the outside world were severed, and the publication of newspapers was suspended for a few days. Gradually, however, the violence subsided, and by 20 May, the situation in Kuala Lumpur, while remaining tense, had largely returned to normal, and it was possible to make a preliminary reckoning.

The official figures relating to the emergency covering the period 13 May to 31 July indicate that 196 persons lost their lives and 180 were wounded by firearms and 259 by other weapons, but these totals have been contested by newspaper correspondents who were at the scene, who maintain that they were much higher. 9,143 persons were arrested, of whom 5,561 were charged in court.[31] 6,000 persons were rendered homeless and at least 211 vehicles destroyed or damaged, and 753 buildings damaged or destroyed by fire.[32]

Many of the older residents of Malaysia who had experienced the Sino-Malay racial disturbances in 1945–6, immediately after the Japanese surrender, considered that it was the worst racial riot in the history of the country.

On 14 May, the Yang di-Pertuan Agong proclaimed a state of national emergency under clause 2 of article 150 of the constitution 'to secure public safety and the maintenance of good order'; the constitution and parliament were suspended, and the elections in East Malaysia were postponed indefinitely.[33]

Two days later, Tunku Abdul Rahman set up a ten-member National Operations Council headed by Tun Abdul Razak, the deputy prime minister, with responsibility for administration under the proclamation of emergency, and appointed a new Cabinet, 'superior to the Operations Council'.[34]

The Tunku made it clear that he remained as prime minister, that he was still in complete overall charge of the country, and that the Operations Council would be responsible to him.[35]

Meanwhile, Tun Tan Siew Sin, (son of Tan Cheng Lock), MCA president, had announced on 13 May that as the MCA had lost the confidence of the Chinese electorate, it would withdraw from the government although it would remain in the Alliance in order to give it a majority. This announcement was made before the outbreak of the riots but it came as a shock as, for the first time since the formation of Malaysia, the Chinese community would not be alongside UMNO and the MIC in the Alliance government. Nevertheless, three MCA members joined the 'Emergency' Cabinet on 20 May.[36]

As the official National Operations Council report on the tragedy says, 'Sino-Malay distrust runs like a thread through the nation's recent history',[37] and since the elected Alliance government had assumed power fifteen years previously, while there had been isolated incidents of Sino-Malay clashes such as those in May 1959 on Pangkor Island; in July 1964 in the Bukit Mertajam district; in July and September 1964 in Singapore; in early 1965 in Kuala Lumpur; and in November 1967 and April 1969 in Penang,[38] there had been nothing on the terrifying scale of the 13 May riots, which are a watershed in contemporary Malaysian history.

In summing up, one may say that the violence which shook Kuala Lumpur was triggered off by the results of the general elections at federal and state levels which saw the Alliance Party, especially the MCA component of it, reeling under body blows from the opposition, but the underlying cause is much deeper and undoubtedly must be looked for in the social, political and economic differences which had grown up between the Chinese and Malays.

Chapter Eight

Aftermath

Why did the 13 May riots occur? Tunku Abdul Rahman placed the blame squarely on the communists and Chinese secret society elements.[1]

However, Tun (Dr.) Ismail, Minister of Home Affairs, seemed to think otherwise, at least, about the communists. 'Everybody thought that the Communists were responsible for the disturbances,' he said. 'Later we found that they were as much surprised as we were.'[2] In a separate statement made soon after the riots, he said, 'Democracy is dead in this country. It died at the hands of the opposition parties who triggered off the events leading to this violence.'[3] Later Chinese secret societies were blamed, then mention was made of 'anti-national and subversive elements'.[4]

But the fact remains, when all is said and done, that in Malay eyes, all of these culprits were Chinese.

The National Operations Council report on the racial disturbances, published on 9 October 1969, which represents the official view, while alluding to the role of the Malayan Communist Party and Chinese secret societies, made play of several other factors. These included differences in the interpretation of the constitution by Malays and non-Malays, and the resentment of 'certain immigrant races'[5] against constitutional provisions relating to Malay special rights and the status accorded to the Malay language, especially under sections 152 and 153 of the constitution. Section 152 provided for the Malay language to be the national language *(Bahasa Malaysia),* and ultimately the sole official language, which meant, of course, that English, Chinese and Tamil would all be relegated to an inferior position. Article 153 covered the responsibility of the Yang di-Pertuan Agong to safeguard the special position of the Malays and the legitimate interests of other communities.

The NOC Report also adverted to the stirring up of racial feelings during the election campaign, presumably by both the Alliance and the opposition parties, and the racial insults and threats which were expressed during the DAP and Gerakan 'victory parades' in Kuala Lumpur.[6]

Although this did not find a place in the NOC Report, there was, too, a reluctance on the part of the younger generation of Chinese to accept the 'bargain' which had been entered into with UMNO by the 'old guard' of the MCA, and Chinese resentment at what they perceived to be the 'Malaysia for the Malays' policy pursued by the Alliance government.

On the Malay side, there was a deep-rooted sense of frustration at being left behind in the modernization process which was taking place in their own country, and a fear that they would be smothered by non-Malays, both numerically and economically. They were determined not to give up their rights and heritage as defined under the constitution lest they should be 'reduced to the status of Red Indians striving to live in the wastelands of America',[7] and probably, unconsciously, there was a reaffirmation of their exclusive sense of community now that Islam, under the constitution, had been granted official recognition as the state religion.

In 1970, the government acknowledged that the riots were caused by 'ethnic polarization and animosity', which is another way of saying that the Malays and Chinese did not get on well together, and by continuing Malay grievances at being at a disadvantage economically compared with the Chinese.[8]

The National Operations Council, which had been delegated executive authority to administer the country, consisted of six Malays and two non-Malays, with Tun Abdul Razak as Director of Operations. The Malay members were Tun (Dr.) Ismail, Minister of Home Affairs; Datuk Hamzah, Minister of Information and Broadcasting; Tan Sri Ghazalie Shafie, Permanent Secretary, Ministry of Foreign Affairs; Tan Sri Abdul Kadir Shamsuddin, Director of Public Services; General Tengku Osman Jiwa, Chief of Staff of the Armed Forces; and Tan Sri Mohammad Salleh, Inspector-General of Police. The Chief Executive Officer was Lieutenant-General Dato Ibrahim. The inclusion of military and police representatives is noteworthy, and as the council came to be involved not only in reestablishing law and order but also in the exercise of wide executive and legislative powers, which normally fall outside the province of the armed forces, it was to lead to rumours later on of the possibility of a military takeover.

The two non-Malay members were Tun Tan Siew Sin, MCA president, and Tun V.T. Sambanthan, MIC president.[9]

The new Emergency Cabinet formed on 20 May 1969 by Tunku Abdul Rahman, as mentioned previously, was superior to the NOC, and Tun Razak had to act on the prime minister's (the Tunku's) advice. The ministers appointed to the cabinet were Tunku Abdul Rahman (Prime Minister); Tun Abdul Razak (Deputy Prime Minister, Defence and acting Finance); Tun (Dr.) Ismail (Home Affairs); Tan Sri Sardon (Health); Mohamed Khir Johari (Commerce and Industry, and acting Local Government and Housing); Tuan Haji Mohamed Ghazali (Agriculture and Cooperatives); Datuk Patinggi Abdul Rahman Haji Ya'akub (Education); Ghafar Baba (National and Rural Development, and Lands and Mines); Hamzah Abu Samah (Information and Broadcasting); Tan Sri Fatimah binte Haji Hashim (Social Welfare); Dato Ganie Gilong (Justice); Tan Sri Temenggong Jugah (Sarawak Affairs); Tun V.T. Sambanthan (Works, Posts and Telecommunications); and V. Manickavasagam (Labour and acting Transport).

The next day it was announced that three MCA members would join the Cabinet as Ministers without Portfolio. They were Tun Tan Siew Sin (former Minister of Finance), Khaw Kai Boh, and Lee Siok Yiew.[10]

It will be recalled that there was a move afoot at the hurriedly called meeting of UMNO campaign directors after the elections to propose that Malay ministers should be appointed to take over the portfolios of Finance and Commerce and Industry and, in this connection, the assumption of Tun Razak and Mohamed Khir Johari of these two portfolios is significant.

In the aftermath of the riots, there had been virtually a breakdown of social and economic contact between the Chinese and Malays. In June, few Chinese and Indians were willing to patronize Malay shops, stalls or hawkers. Non-Malays refused to ride in taxis driven by Malays, buy *batik* cloth, or even eat durians, which were regarded as 'Malay' fruit. There was still 'bad blood' between the two races. In the background, the more vocal Malays were struggling to assume control of UMNO so that they could prevent UMNO from making concessions. 'There is no denying the fact that there is a struggle for power going on inside UMNO', the Tunku commented, 'as between those who built the Party and helped in our independence and the new elements, the "Ultras".'[11]

On 12 June 1969, it was officially announced that all non-citizens were required to obtain work permits even if they were permanent residents of the country, and aliens would be granted work permits only if there were not sufficient qualified *bumiputras* to fill the jobs.[12] In November 1969, all citizens (i.e. non-Malays) issued citizenship certificates under section 30 of the constitution, that is, on the grounds that one of their parents was a citizen or domiciled in the country at the time of their birth, were required to submit their citizenship papers to the authorities for checking to make sure that they were not obtained under false pretences. Only 95,540 such certificates were cleared by March 1971, and 181,160 non-Malays had their citizenship revoked or were left holding invalid citizenship certificates.[13]

On 30 July 1969 the Minister of Education announced a plan to introduce Bahasa Malaysia in stages, starting from Primary One in 1970, as the main medium of instruction in Peninsular Malaysia schools. English was to be taught only as a second language. On this time-scale, by 1982 all secondary education, including Form Six would be in the medium of Bahasa Malaysia, and beyond that, starting in 1983, Bahasa Malaysia would be the medium of instruction in first-year university classes, and would be introduced progressively year by year until all university classes would use Bahasa Malaysia as the medium of instruction, except for teaching foreign languages.[14]

The reasoning behind this was that Malay was regarded as the means to create national unity. While it was conceded that English was widely spoken in Malaysia, it was considered to be 'elitist', and national dignity dictated that an autochthonous language should be given pride of place. Chinese and Tamil were, in this sense, not thought of as being indigenous languages, and their continued use was regarded as only tending to encourage polarization of the various communities.[15]

On 18 June 1969, Tunku Abdul Rahman received what he described as a 'scurrilous' letter[16] from Dr. Mahathir bin Mohamad, an UMNO candidate who was defeated in the federal elections, and a member of UMNO's supreme council, accusing the Tunku of being pro-Chinese, and demanding his resignation as prime minister. This letter was leaked to the press so that it received the widest possible publicity. University of Malaya students demonstrated on the university campus calling for the Tunku's resignation on the grounds that he was not taking a strong enough line with the Chinese over such matters as education and language, and that he had failed to improve the economic position of the Malays.[17] There was a spate of vicious letters which were just as much anti-Tunku as they were anti-Chinese.

Dr. Mahathir Mohamad, a medical practitioner with a private practice in Kedah, was the most prominent of a group of relatively young UMNO intellectuals who believed that not enough was being done for the Malays. Another name mentioned in this connection was Musa Hitam (later Datuk), who had recently been appointed as an Assistant Minister to Tun Abdul Razak.

The 'Young Turks' worked closely with persons such as Tan Sri Ja'afar Albar and Tan Sri Syed Nasir, who were considered by many to belong to the 'ultras' camp.[18] Both the 'Young Turks' and the 'ultras' were reported to be anti-Tunku Abdul Rahman and his supporters, and as Malay nationalists they had a reputation for being uncompromising towards non-Malays.

At this time, a lecturer in Malay Studies at the University of Malaya, Raja Mukhtaruddin Dain, came to notice for circulating a leaflet entitled 'Message to the Malays', which was banned under the Internal Security Act, together with the other documents referred to above, for fear of exacerbating a situation which was already tense, and which could easily lead to a further outbreak of violence.

It was clear that some UMNO members wanted to impose one-party rule and exclude the Chinese completely from the government.

It was just as well for the Chinese that all these pressures were resisted. Dr. Mahathir was expelled from UMNO for breach of party discipline, Musa Hitam was dismissed from his post as assistant minister, and sent on 'study leave' to Britain, and the police held the university students in check.[19]

'The ultras believe in the wild and fantastic theory of absolute dominion by one race over the other communities regardless of the Constitution', Tun (Dr.) Ismail said over Television Malaysia on 2 August 1969. 'The moderates under the leadership of the Tunku firmly hold the view that in the Malaysian multiracial society, such a theory is not just a harmless pipe dream but an extremely dangerous fantasy.

'Polarization has taken place in Malaysian politics and the extreme racialists among the ruling party are making a desperate bid to topple the present leadership.

'I must warn the extremists and others as well, that if the anti-Tunku campaigns or activities are carried out in such a manner ... as to cause undue fear and alarm among members of any community ... I will not hesitate to exercise my powers under the law against those responsible....'[20]

Then the Tunku lambasted the 'ultras' and extremists in no uncertain fashion. 'Firstly I am a Malay,' he said, 'and naturally I am their leader. But I have to see to the interests of the non-Malays too. We just cannot throw them into the sea.'[21]

The turning point came when the General Officer Commanding, Peninsular Malaysia, took an oath on 2 August 1969 on behalf of his officers and men to pledge loyalty to and support for the Tunku and his government.[22]

This may well have saved the day both for the Tunku and his supporters (as well as the Chinese), because at that time, when parliament was suspended and a state of emergency had been declared, in the final analysis, power rested with the military, and whoever controlled the military, controlled the country.

The Tunku survived as a multiracial symbol, and a positive step was made to patch up the differences between the three main races making up Malaysia, by the establishment of three new institutions. In July 1969, National Goodwill Councils came into existence all over Malaysia with various local committees. The president was the Tunku who started a six-week, nation-wide tour by visiting Penang, where the state government was in the hands of Gerakan, with Dr Lim Chong Eu as chief minister. Malays, Chinese and Indians could talk to each other again and a start was made to restore an intercommunal dialogue.[23]

In January 1970, the Department of National Unity and the National Consultative Council came into being; they were more formal and had official links with the NOC.[24] The National Consultative Council was foreshadowed in the National Operations Council's Report wherein it was stated that 'it is intended after the publication of this Report to invite representatives of various groups in the country — political, religious, economic and others — to serve on a Consultative Council, where issues affecting our national unity will be discussed fully and frankly....'[25]

Its task was to determine 'permanent solutions to our racial problems to ensure that the May 13 tragedy does not recur'.[26] It met periodically over the next eighteen months.

In some ways, the National Consultative Council was the *alter ego* of parliament, which was waiting in the wings, and it was by no means certain that when parliament was reconvened the NCC would necessarily disappear (see below).

It was a multiracial body consisting of 65 members representing federal and state governments, political parties (with the exception of DAP and Party Rakyat), and functional groups, who were encouraged to speak frankly on matters of national importance such as racial issues and national unity.

The NOC Report had already pointed out the way Sino-Malay friction could be met. 'Citizens of this country,' it said, 'especially those who became citizens by virtue of the provisions that started with the Federation of Malaya Agreement, 1948, leading to the Merdeka Constitution, 1957, should understand the significance of the entrenched provisions of the Constitution. Malaysians, despite their ethnic origins, should appreciate the potential and distinctiveness of their country. The guidelines will be provided by the newly-formed Department of National Unity and the National Operations Council.'[27]

The intention to prepare guidelines in the shape of a national ideology was announced by Tan Sri Ghazali in mid-July 1969. The drafting was done by the Department of National Unity headed by Ghazali, and the final draft was submitted to the National Consultative Council for approval.[28]

On 31 August 1970, the thirteenth anniversary of Merdeka, the Yang di-Pertuan Agong formally promulgated the statement of national ideology which was called the *Rukunegara*. While *'rukun'* certainly has Islamic undertones about it, and may be translated as 'fundamental doctrine, commandment, or essential part of a religion', as brought out by Means and Milne and Mauzy,[29] it is indeed very appropriate in the context of interracial relations, as it means, too, 'quiet and peaceful', 'like the ideal relationship of friendship', 'without quarrel or strife', and 'united in purpose while mutually helping each other'.[30] *'Negara'* means nation.

As the Malaysian government intends to use the *Rukunegara* as the basic model for its strategy to bring about national unity, and the principles enunciated in it are meant to serve as a bond to bind together the various strands of Malaysia's multiracial society, it may be of interest to reproduce it here:

'Our Nation, MALAYSIA, is dedicated —
To achieving a greater unity for all her peoples;
To maintaining a democratic way of life;
To creating a just society in which the wealth of the nation shall be equitably distributed;
To ensuring a liberal approach to her rich and diverse cultural traditions;
To building a progressive society which shall be orientated to modern science and technology.
We, her peoples, pledge our united efforts to attain these ends guided by these principles —
Belief in God (*Kepercayaan kepada Tuhan*)
Loyalty to King and Country (*Kesetiaan kepada Raja dan Negara*)
Upholding the Constitution (*Keluhuran Perlembagaan*)
Rule of Law (*Kedaulatan Undang-undang*)
Good Behaviour and Morality (*Kesopanan dan Kesusilaan*).'

The following commentary elucidating the meaning of these five principles accompanied the declaration:

1 Islam is the official religion of the Federation. Other religions and beliefs may be practised in peace and harmony and there shall be no discrimination against any citizen on the ground of religion.

2 The loyalty that is expected of every citizen is that he must be faithful and bear true allegiance to His Majesty the Yang di-Pertuan Agong....

3 It is the duty of a citizen to respect and appreciate the letter, the spirit and the historical background of the Constitution. This historical background led to such provisions as those regarding the position of ... the Rulers, the position of Islam as the official religion, the position of Malays and other Natives, the legitimate interests of other communities, and conferment of citizenship. It is the sacred duty of a citizen to defend and uphold the Constitution.

4 Justice is founded upon the rule of law. Every citizen is equal before the law. Fundamental liberties are guaranteed to all citizens. These include liberty of the person, equal protection of the law, freedom of religion, rights of property and protection against banishment. The Constitution confers on a citizen the right of free speech, assembly and association and this right may be enjoyed freely subject only to limitations imposed by law.

5 Individuals and groups shall conduct their affairs in such a manner as not to violate any of the accepted canon of behaviour which is arrogant or offensive to the sensitivities of any group. No citizen should question the loyalty of another citizen on the ground that he belongs to a particular community.[31]

In the circumstances, non-Malays could take heart that the *Rukunegara* steered a middle path through the tangled skein of Sino-Malay relations. A clear hint was given in it to Malay 'ultras' and racial extremists that they were not going to have things entirely their own way, and that parliamentary democracy was to continue and a totalitarian form of government was not envisaged. The Chinese were reassured that there would be no threat to their culture ('ensuring a liberal approach to her (Malaysia's) rich and diverse cultural traditions'), and the direction in which education would be pointed was indicated ('a progressive society which shall be oriented to modern science and technology').

The third principle, 'upholding the Constitution', made it clear that the Chinese would have to accept Malay as the national language and the sole official language, as well as accept the 'special position' of the *bumiputras* and the legitimate interests of other communities. However, the fifth principle was in favour of the Chinese — 'no citizen should question the loyalty of another citizen on the ground that he belongs to a particular community'.

The *Rukunegara* was supported by all legal political parties, and its principles became widely known and were often referred to and quoted.

At the time of the promulgation of the *Rukunegara,* Tunku Abdul Rahman had announced that he intended to retire from the premiership which he had held since independence, and on 22 September 1970 he formally submitted his resignation to the Yang di-Pertuan Agong, and Tun Abdul Razak assumed office.

At the same time that he had announced his retirement, the Tunku had remarked on the government's intention to lift the suspension on parliament and the various state legislatures in February 1971.

Tun Razak appointed Tun (Dr.) Ismail as Deputy Prime Minister, and Datuk Hussein Onn, who was his brother-in-law, left his private law practice at Tun Razak's request to serve the nation as Minister of Education. The MCA abandoned its decision not to participate in the government, and Tun Tan Siew Sin returned as Minister of Finance.[32]

Once again the Alliance Party was at the helm, made up as before of three communal parties, UMNO, the MCA and the MIC, although it was now geared toward a new strategy to meet the interrelated problems of the economic deprivation of the Malays and the hostility and ill-feeling which was keeping the

Malays and Chinese apart.

The ban on party politics was withdrawn but only after the NOC, with the full support of the National Consultative Council, amended the Sedition Act to make it an offence to question publicly the powers and privileges of the Yang di-Pertuan Agong or the Malay rulers, the citizenship law, the use of Malay as the sole national and official language, the 'special position' and rights of the *bumiputras,* and the status of Islam as the state religion.[33]

On 23 February 1971, the new parliament was opened, marking the end of twenty months of rule by NOC decree. The new prime minister, Tun Abdul Razak, addressed the Dewan Rakyat as follows:

'Mr Speaker, we meet today some twenty months late. I regret this as much as any Member of this House, but we all know why this had to be. The disturbances of May 1969 mark the darkest period in our national history ... Today life has generally returned to normal ... (but) if we do not take precautions now, we shall stand condemned before our people as failing in our duty ....'

Tun Abdul Razak opined that the only way to avoid a recurrence of the trouble was to restructure the whole economy so as to eradicate poverty for all Malaysians, irrespective of race, and to correct racial economic imbalance by increasing the participation of *bumiputras* in the economic life of the country.[34]

Tun Razak made it quite clear that the return to parliamentary government was contingent upon parliament passing the Constitution (Amendment) Bill which was designed to confirm the NOC decree amending the Sedition Act which made it an offence to discuss publicly 'sensitive racial issues', and not only that, but to remove parliamentary privilege in regard to the discussion of these topics both at federal and state levels.

The Constitution (Amendment) Bill also granted additional power to the Yang di-Pertuan Agong to direct post-secondary institutions to reserve certain proportions of places for Malays in selected courses of study where the numbers of Malays were disproportionately small, such as medicine, engineering and science.

After several days of debate — the MCA supported the Bill but it was opposed by the DAP and the PPP — the amendments to the constitution were passed by the Dewan Rakyat by a vote of 126 to 17. The other House, the Dewan Negara (Senate), passed it unanimously.[35]

With the resumption of parliamentary rule, the NOC continued as the National Security Council, under the leadership of Prime Minister Tun Abdul Razak. The National Consultative Council and the National Goodwill Council were amalgamated to form a new multiracial advisory body called the 'National Unity Council'. This new council had the task of advising the prime minister on the sensitive racial issues, which were banned from parliamentary and public debate, and undertaking research in race relations.

In a sense, the new economic policy announced by Tun Abdul Razak at the opening of Parliament was not entirely new. It will be recollected that General Templer, soon after his arrival as High Commissioner of the Federation of Malaya in February 1952, had made reference to the necessity for the Malays 'to play a full part in the economic life of the country' (see Chapter Six). However, for the most part, in the *First Malaysia Plan 1966—70*, the adjusting of the economic balance between the Malay and Chinese communities was thought of in terms of developing the rural areas of the country, where most of the Malays were found, as opposed to the urban areas, which were predominantly Chinese settlements and schemes for land settlements benefiting the Malays were thereupon devised by the government or quasi-government organizations mentioned in Chapter Six, such as FELDA, RIDA and MARA.

Nevertheless, it was reasoned that the efforts of these bodies were inadequate, and that too little was being done for the Malays, otherwise the Malays would not have been still labouring under a sense of economic deprivation which led to the 13 May 1969 riots,[36] and it was with this in mind that a new economic development plan, the *Second Malaysia Plan 1971—1975* (SMP) was drawn up, and published on 25 June 1971, with further details and statistics being provided in the *Mid-Term Review of the Second Malaysia Plan 1971—1975*, published on 20 November 1973. It was followed in 1976 by the *Third Malaysia Plan 1976—1980*.

The aims of the New Economic Policy (NEP) were given in the introduction of the SMP. 'The Plan incorporates a two-pronged New Economic Policy for development. The first prong is to reduce and eventually eradicate poverty, by raising income levels and increasing employment opportunities for all Malaysians, irrespective of race. The second prong aims at accelerating the process of restructuring Malaysian society to correct economic imbalance, so as to reduce and eventually eliminate the identification of race with economic function. This process involves the modernisation of rural life, a rapid and balanced growth of urban activities and the creation of a Malay commercial and industrial community in all categories and at all levels of operation, so that Malays and other indigenous people will become full partners in all respects of the economic life of the nation.'[37]

The 'first prong' of the NEP was to be achieved by comprehensive policies of economic growth and development which would improve the lot of all Malaysians, regardless of race. But, in practice, most of the specific measures to be taken for the eradication of poverty affected the Malays, either in agriculture or in assisting their movement from the traditional to the modern sector of the economy.

The strategy to be adopted for the 'second prong', that is, the restructuring of Malaysian society to correct economic imbalance, was more far-reaching as it covered a wide range of programmes to enable *bumiputras* to participate in the dynamic sectors of the economy.

The *Mid-Term Review* stated that there would be an increased scale of activities in agriculture and rural development, commerce and industry, transport and the social sectors.[38]

With reference to restructuring wealth ownership (see Appendix 6), foreign interests accounted for 60 per cent of the total share capital in the corporate sector, and Chinese ownership accounted for about 22 per cent or just under 60 per cent of the total Malaysian share. In industries in which foreign interests were not supreme, Chinese ownership of share capital topped the list amounting to between 40—50 per cent. *Bumiputra* ownership of share capital, on the other hand, was a mere 2 per cent of the overall total.

The target laid down to achieve a more balanced pattern in the ownership of assets in all sectors of the economy was that within a period of 20 years, *bumiputras* would own and manage at least 30 per cent of the total commercial and industrial activities of the economy in all categories and scales of operations, as related in Chapter Six.

There was great difficulty in finding sufficient *bumiputra* capital to take up the shares, but the government proposed to overcome this by acquiring shares directly by government institutions and holding them in trust for *bumiputras* until they were in a position to purchase them with their own capital.[39]

It was decided that the employment pattern at all levels should reflect more closely the racial composition of the population (see Appendix 1). For most industries, a 40 per cent quota figure was set for the employment of Malay staff although this obviously depended on the availability of suitably trained and qualified Malay personnel.[40]

Manufacturing was to be the command sector in the expansion of the Malaysian economy, and special attention was to be paid to the creation of a Malay commercial and industrial community.[41] The government's policy was to 'bring industry to the Malays' rather than the other way round, and labour intensive industrial projects which provided new employment opportunities in the rural areas were to be started.[42] These 'growth poles' in the rural areas were to be enhanced by the provision of such amenities as schools, housing, electricity, medical centres, transportation and communications.

The prime minister appealed to Malays to go into business and not necessarily to aim at 'safe', comfortable jobs in government service, and to pay more attention to science and technology, while not departing from the tenets of their faith.[43]

It was hoped to bring into being a Malay entrepreneurial community 'within one generation' and, as an incentive, *bumiputra* contractors were assured of being granted at least a certain percentage of government and quasi-government contracts.[44]

But by 1970, the number of *bumiputras* in the commercial sector was still disappointingly small and amounted to only around 24 per cent of the total number of persons employed, and a Sino-Malay Economic Cooperation Advisory Board which was set up soon after the 13 May 1969 racial riots to encourage joint ventures between Chinese and Malay businessmen came to nothing.[45]

It seemed that in joint Sino-Malay business ventures, the Malay partner was often inclined to assume the role of a 'sleeping partner', with his participation limited to obtaining licences, quotas or tenders from the government, and allowing his Chinese partner to take over from there and run the business. This was known as an 'Ali-Baba' operation: 'Ali' standing for the Malay and 'Baba' for the Chinese.

Actually, this was quite understandable, as there were very few Malays with business experience and know-how, who felt at home in the world of finance and business, as traditionally Malays attached greater prestige to working in the government sector, even though it might be only as a clerical worker or a peon (office-boy).

The government or quasi-government agencies and corporations had a more important function to perform in the NEP than they had under the *First Malaysia Plan,* and the *Mid-Term Review of the Second Malaysia Plan* is replete with acronyms such as MARA *(Majlis Amanah Ra'ayat* or Council of Trust for the Indigenous People), PERNAS *(Perbadanan Nasional* or State Trading Corporation), UDA (Urban Development Authority) and SEDC (State Economic Development Corporation). All these bodies were formed by the government to assist and to guide *bumiputras* to play a fuller part in the economic life of post-13 May 1969 Malaysia, and were all part of the grand strategy 'to restructure Malaysian society' in order 'to correct racial economic imbalance', in the context of an expanding economy, and 'to reduce and eventually eliminate the identification of race with economic function'.[46]

The long-term plan was to hand over the business enterprises started by these agencies to *bumiputras,* although when and how this would be effected was not made clear in the SMP. In this connection, it will be recollected that by 1971 MARA had formed and handed over some bus services to Malay concerns (see Chapter Six).

Education as a 'tool for restructuring society' was another matter accorded priority in the SMP. Mention has been made earlier of the Constitution (Amendment) Bill which gave the paramount ruler power to direct universities and other institutions of higher learning to admit more *bumiputras,* even though their educational qualifications might be lower than that of non-Malay candidates, especially in the fields of medicine, engineering and science. However, there were problems. While the University of Malaya at Kuala Lumpur was able to expand its physical facilities to take in the increased enrolment, Universiti Kebangsaan Malaysia (National University of Malaysia) and Universiti Sains Malaysia, did not have either sufficient facilities or teachers to do so. There were 8,052 students at the University of Malaya in the 1970–1 session. Of these 1,363 were in Science, 631 in Medicine, 392 in Engineering and 324 in Agriculture. Universiti Sains, Penang, began with an intake of 60 science students in 1969 and by 1970–1 the enrolment had increased to 262.[47] Universiti Kebangsaan Malaysia was established in May 1970 with an intake of 191 students. It was the first university in the country to use Malay as the medium of instruction.[48]

With the reconvening of parliament on 23 February 1971, it appeared to be tacitly accepted by both Malays and Chinese that to question the assumptions of the NEP would only open old wounds and, in any case, the government repeatedly emphasized that in the implementation of the NEP it would ensure that 'no particular group will experience any loss or feel any sense of deprivation'.[49] This had to be accepted at its face value and a chance given to see whether the new strategies to promote national unity would work.

What of the position then, of the Chinese after the bloody 13 May 1969 disturbances? The 'bargain' which had been entered into by the MCA and UMNO prior to independence in 1957 aimed at creating a balance which would be adhered to by both Chinese and Malays. This had been shattered during the 13 May 1969 riots. What are the prospects of the two main communities in Malaysia working out a *modus vivendi?* There are many barriers which have persisted since the Chinese first started to immigrate to Malaya in large numbers in the second half of the nineteenth century. For instance, they do not share a common history, heritage or culture, and even their language, dress, food, daily habits, religious beliefs and economic pursuits are different. They do not 'dream the same dreams'.

By 1971, it appeared that there were three options open to the Chinese in a Malayan-Malaysia. They could be assimilated, depending on whether they agreed to turn themselves into Malays, or they could be integrated into Malaysian society to form a *suku* (literally 'a quarter' or 'a group'), that is, a Chinese-Malaysian and not a Malaysian-Chinese *suku,* which would nevertheless be part of the racial mosaic making up Malaysia, in the same way that Malaysia includes the separate ethnic groups of Sabah and Sarawak, such as, the Melanaus, Ibans (Sea Dayaks), Land Dayaks, Dusuns, Muruts and Bajaus. Or they could remain separate and outside the mainstream of Malaysian life, in which case further friction could be expected which would inevitably lead to further outbreaks of racial violence, and perhaps rend the country asunder.

It appears unlikely that the Chinese will accept the first option, bearing in mind their intense pride in their culture. Even in Thailand where the Chinese and Thais come from the same stock, and there are no religious barriers between the two races, assimilation is by no means complete. In any case, in Malaysia, Islam would present an insuperable obstacle, since there can be no compromise over this, and it constitutes the main reason why Malaysia, with its multiracial society, has not become the melting pot of Asia. The third option is unthinkable, and even the most chauvinistic Chinese realizes that it would not be possible for the Chinese to remain as a separate enclave in a Malay-oriented Malaysia.

Integration would therefore seem to offer the best solution,[50] and it would be quite acceptable in the context of the *Rukunegara* where, as has been noted earlier, reference has been made to Malaysia's 'rich and diverse cultural traditions'. Also, the NEP, if it is accepted to mean what it says, makes it quite clear that the government 'will spare no efforts to promote national unity and develop a just and progressive Malaysian society in a rapidly expanding economy so that no one will experience any loss or feel any sense of deprivation of his rights, privileges, income, job or opportunity'.[51]

Meanwhile, while the frequent verbal battles between the two main component parties of the ruling political alliance, namely, UMNO and MCA, must indeed give rise to widespread anxiety, there is no doubt that the government's language and education policies provide the key to the problem. Although they were initially firmly resisted by the Chinese, if they come to be accepted, they will eventually result in producing Chinese-Malaysians[52] educated through the medium of Bahasa Malaysia (the national language) and having a Malaysian outlook, even though this may take some years to achieve, and the way ahead may be tortuous.

Appendix 1

RACIAL COMPOSITION OF MALAYA FROM 1835 TO 1970 BY PERCENTAGES

Racial Group	*1835*	*1884*	*1921*	*1931*	*1947*	*1957*	*1965*	*1970*
Malays	85.9	63.9	54.0	49.2	49.5	49.8	50.1	53.2
Chinese	7.7	29.4	29.4	33.9	38.4	37.2	36.8	35.4
Indians	—	—	15.1	15.1	10.8	11.3	11.1	10.6
Others	6.3	6.7	1.5	1.8	1.3	1.8	2.0	0.8

Source: Compiled from Alvin Rabushka, *Race and Politics in Urban Malaya,* p. 21, and S. Husin Ali, *Malay Peasant Society and Leadership,* p. 23.

NOTES:

The figures for 1921, 1931, 1947, 1957, 1965 and 1970 refer to Peninsular Malaysia only.

The category 'Malays' includes all persons of Malay, Indonesian or aboriginal ethnic origin.

Pakistanis and Ceylonese are counted with 'Indians'.

The figures given for 'Others' in 1835 and 1884 are made up mainly of Indians and Pakistanis.

Appendix 2

ABSTRACT FROM 1931 CENSUS

	Area	Malays	% of Total	Chinese	% of Total	Indians	% of Total
Singapore	217	71,177	12.5	421,821	74.3	51,019	9.0
Penang	388	118,832	33.1	176,518	49.0	58,020	16.1
Malacca	720	95,307	51.0	65,179	34.9	23,238	12.4
Straits Settlements	1,325	285,316	25.6	663,518	59.6	132,277	11.9
Perak	7,983	272,546	35.6	325,527	42.5	159,152	20.8
Selangor	3,156	122,868	23.1	241,351	45.3	155,924	29.2
Negri Sembilan	2,550	87,195	37.3	92,371	39.5	50,100	21.4
Pahang	14,000	111,122	61.7	52,291	29.0	14,820	8.2
FMS	27,689	593,731	34.7	711,540	41.5	379,996	22.2
Johore	7,500	234,422	46.4	215,076	41.4	51,038	10.1
Kedah	3,800	286,262	66.6	78,415	18.2	50,824	12.0
Perlis	316	39,831	80.9	6,500	13.2	966	2.0
Kelantan	5,870	330,774	91.2	17,612	4.9	6,752	1.9
Trengganu	6,000	164.564	91.5	13,254	7.4	1,371	0.8
UMS	23,486	1,055,853	69.2	330,857	21.7	110,951	7.3
Brunei	2,500	26,972	89.5	2,683	8.9	377	1.3
Unlocated		149	10.0	794	53.1	408	27.3
Malaya	55,000	1,962,021	44.7	1,709,392	39.0	624,009	14.2

Source: Rupert Emerson, *Malaysia, A Study in Direct and Indirect Rule*, p. 22.

Appendix 3

RACES ENGAGED IN PRINCIPAL OCCUPATIONS 1931

Occupation	Europeans	Malays	Immigrant Malaysians	Chinese	Indians
Fishermen	—	5,715	307	7,291	56
Rice Planters	—	78,009	11,113	1,038	1,892
Rubber Estate Owners, Managers, etc.	1,121	1,803	910	1,514	58
Others in Rubber Cultivation	—	27,618	20,825	100,789	131,099
Coconut Estate Owners, Managers, etc.	11	744	669	23	9
Others in Coconut Cultivation	—	4,262	5,982	1,256	8,010
Unclassified and Multifarious Agriculture	23	18,168	7,381	16,115	9,883
Tin Mine Owners, Managers, etc.	48	8	—	214	—
Others in Tin Mining	282	543	465	70,704	4,622
Proprietors and Managers of Business	246	475	574	16,894	4,428
Salesmen, Shop Assistants, etc.	144	541	105	16,576	3,790

Source: Rupert Emerson, *Malaysia, A Study in Direct and Indirect Rule*, p. 183.

Appendix 4

PARLIAMENTARY ELECTIONS: SEATS WON AND VOTES POLLED BY PARTIES (TOTAL)

Parties	Seats Won			Seats Contested			Votes polled — % of the total		
	1959	1964	1969	1959	1964	1969	1959	1964	1969
1. Alliance									
UMNO	52	59	51	70	68	67	35.94	38.14	33.67
MCA	19	27	13	31	33	33	14.82	18.68	13.50
MIC	3	3	2	3	3	3	1.02	1.55	1.24
	74	89	66	104	104	103	51.78	58.37	48.41
2. Democratic Action Party									
Malay Candidates	n.a.	—	—	n.a.	—	1	n.a.	—	0.32
Non-Malay Candidates	n.a.	1	13	n.a.	11	23	n.a.	2.06	13.41
	—	1	13	—	11	24	—	2.06	13.73
3. Gerakan Rakyat Malaysia									
Malay Candidates	n.a.	n.a.	1	n.a.	n.a.	3	n.a.	n.a.	2.14
Non-Malay Candidates	n.a.	n.a.	7	n.a.	n.a.	11	n.a.	n.a.	6.43
	—	—	8	—	—	14	—	—	8.57
4. People's Progressive Party									
Malay Candidates	—	—	—	1	1	—	0.04	0.06	—
Non-Malay Candidates	4	2	4	18	8	6	6.26	3.59	3.87
	4	2	4	19	9	6	6.30	3.65	3.87
5. Pan-Malayan Islamic Party	13	9	12	58	52	59	21.27	14.45	23.75
6. Parti Rakyat	—	—	—	—	—	5	—	—	1.24
7. Independents	3	—	—	27	8	2	4.76	0.66	0.34

Parties	Seats Won 1959	Seats Won 1964	Seats Won 1969	Seats Contested 1959	Seats Contested 1964	Seats Contested 1969	Votes polled — % of the total 1959	Votes polled — % of the total 1964	Votes polled — % of the total 1969
8. Socialist Front									
Malay Candidates	1	—	n.a.	11	30	n.a.	2.86	6.02	n.a.
Non-Malay Candidates	7	2	n.a.	27	33	n.a.	10.06	10.13	n.a.
	8	2	—	38	63	—	12.92	16.15	—
9. United Democratic Party									
Malay Candidates	n.a.	—	n.a.	n.a.	8	n.a.	n.a.	0.56	n.a.
Non-Malay Candidates	n.a.	1	n.a.	n.a.	19	n.a.	n.a.	3.74	n.a.
	—	1	—	—	27	—	—	4.30	—
10. Parti Negara	1	—	n.a.	9	4	n.a.	2.11	0.36	n.a.
11. Malayan Party	1	—	n.a.	2	—	n.a.	0.86	—	n.a.
	104	104	103[a]	257	278	213	100.00	100.00	99.91[b]

[a]Election in 1 constituency postponed.
[b]0.09 per cent of total polled by United Malaysian Chinese Organization in Negri Sembilan.
n.a. = Not applicable

Source: R.K. Vasil, *The Malaysian General Election of 1969*, p. 85.

Appendix 5

STATE ELECTIONS: SEATS WON AND VOTES POLLED BY PARTIES (TOTAL)

	Seats Won			*Seats Contested*			*Votes polled — % of the total*		
Parties	*1959*	*1964*	*1969*	*1959*	*1964*	*1969*	*1959*	*1964*	*1969*
1. Alliance									
UMNO	140	164	133	191	189	187	36.98	37.70	33.50
MCA	59	67	26	78	82	80	16.29	17.39	12.71
MIC	7	10	3	13	11	10	2.25	2.53	1.74
	206	241	162	282	282	277	55.52	57.62	47.95
2. Democratic Action Party									
Malay Candidates	n.a.	—	2	n.a.	—	9	n.a.	—	1.28
Non-Malay Candidates	n.a.	—	29	n.a.	15	48	n.a.	0.90	10.48
	—	—	31	—	15	57	—	0.90	11.76
3. Gerakan Rakyat Malaysia									
Malay Candidates	n.a	n.a.	2	n.a.	n.a.	9	n.a.	n.a.	0.97
Non-Malay Candidates	n.a.	n.a.	24	n.a.	n.a.	28	n.a.	n.a.	7.81
	—	—	26	—	—	37	—	—	8.78
4. People's Progressive Party									
Malay Candidates	1	—	1	4	3	2	0.64	0.21	0.30
Non-Malay Candidates	7	5	11	35	23	14	5.11	4.30	4.49
	8	5	12	39	26	16	5.75	4.51	4.79
5. Pan-Malayan Islamic Party	43	25	40	200	158	179	20.80	15.25	22.80
6. Parti Rakyat	*a*	*a*	3	*a*	*a*	37	*a*	*a*	1.53
7. Independents	5	—	3	76	39	38	3.61	1.09	2.29

Parties	Seats Won 1959	Seats Won 1964	Seats Won 1969	Seats Contested 1959	Seats Contested 1964	Seats Contested 1969	Votes polled — % of the total 1959	Votes polled — % of the total 1964	Votes polled — % of the total 1969
8. Socialist Front									
Malay Candidates	1	—	n.a	76	77	n.a.	3.76	4.83	n.a.
Non-Malay Candidates	15	7	n.a.	48	90	n.a.	5.95	11.47	n.a.
	16	7	—	124	167	—	9.71	16.30	—
9. United Democratic Party									
Malay Candidates	n.a.	—	n.a.	n.a.	28	n.a.	n.a.	1.01	n.a.
Non-Malay Candidates	n.a.	4	n.a.	n.a.	36	n.a.	n.a.	2.93	n.a.
	—	4	—	—	64	—	—	3.94	—
10. Parti Negara	4	—	n.a.	96	17	n.a.	4.29	0.39	n.a.
11. Malayan Party	—	—	n.a.	6	—	n.a.	0.32	—	n.a.
	282	282	277	823	768	641	100.00	100.00	99.90[b]

[a]During 1959 and 1965 Parti Rakyat was a member of the Socialist Front and therefore votes polled by it are included in the Socialist Front vote.

[b]0.10 per cent of the total polled by the United Malaysian Chinese Organization in Negri Sembilan.

n.a. = Not applicable

Source: R.K. Vasil, *The Malaysian General Election of 1969*, p. 73.

Appendix 6

OWNERSHIP OF SHARE CAPITAL OF LIMITED COMPANIES, BY RACE AND SECTOR, PENINSULAR MALAYSIA, 1970

	Malay		*Chinese*		*Indian*		*Foreign*		*Total* [1]
	(M$5000)	%	*(M$5000)*	%	*(M$5000)*	%	*(M$5000)*	%	*(M$5000)*
Agriculture, forestry and fisheries	13,724	0.9	177,438	22.4	16,191	0.1	1,079,715	75.3	1,432,400
Mining and quarrying	3,876	0.7	91,557	16.8	2,488	0.4	393,910	72.4	543,497
Manufacturing	33,650	2.5	296,363	22.0	8,880	0.7	804,282	59.6	1,348,245
Construction	1,258	2.2	30,855	52.8	447	0.8	19,937	34.1	58,419
Transport and communications	10,875	13.3	35,498	43.4	1,903	2.3	9,845	12.0	81,887
Commerce	4,715	0.8	184,461	30.4	4,711	0.7	384,549	63.5	605,164
Banking and insurance	21,164	3.3	155,581	24.3	4,434	0.6	332,790	52.2	636,850
Others	13,349	2.3	220,330	37.8	13,348	2.3	182,862	31.4	582,516
Total	102,611	1.9	1,192,083	22.5	52,402	1.0	3,207,890	60.7	5,288,978

[1] The total includes share capital ownership by Federal and State Governments and Statutory Bodies and other Malaysian residents (individuals and nominee and locally controlled companies), amounting to about $734 million. In this Table, the racial shares in each sector exclude these two groups.

Source: *Mid-Term Review of the Second Malaysia Plan 1971—1975*, p. 82.

Appendix 7

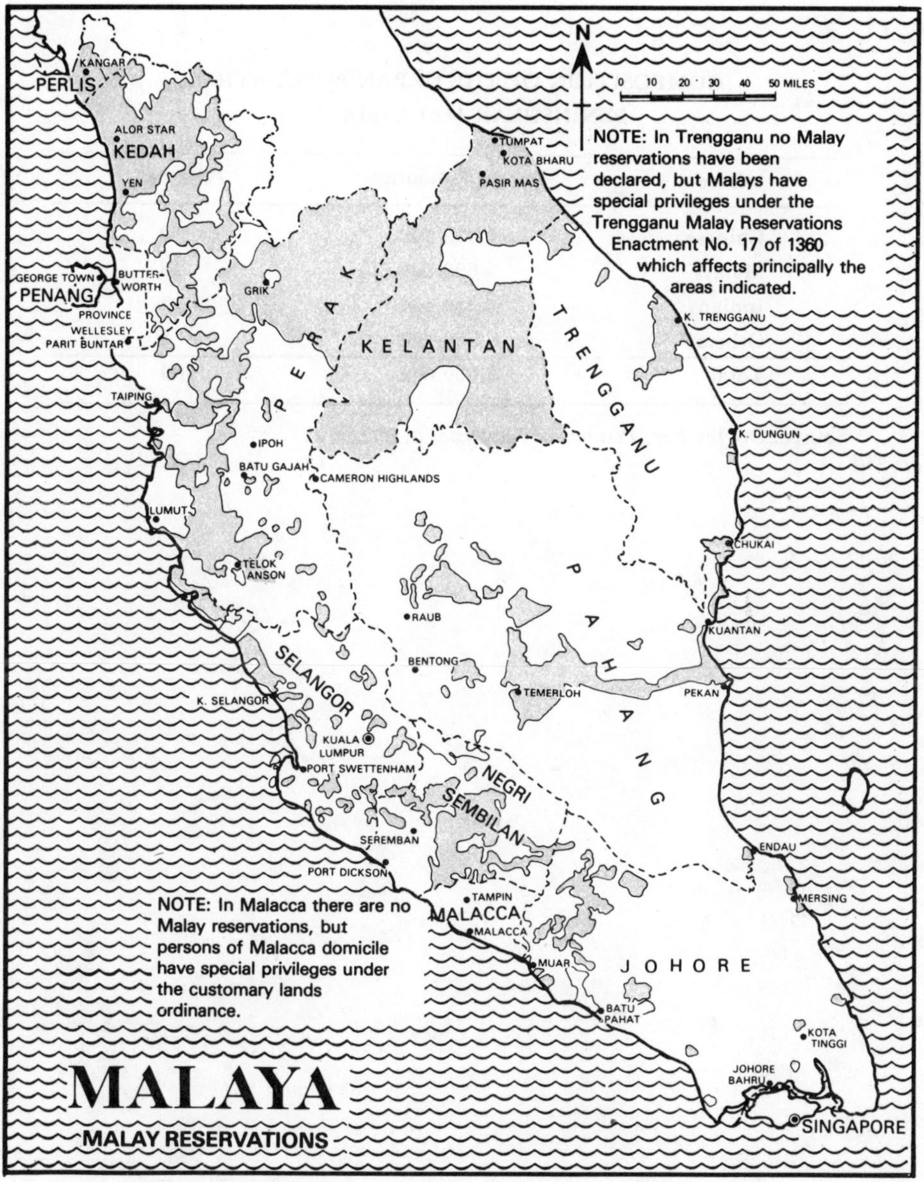

Source: *The Economic Development of Malaya*, Map 7, p. 226.

Appendix 8

COMPOSITION OF THE URBAN POPULATION, PENINSULAR MALAYSIA, 1970

Race	*Urban Population*	*Per Cent*
Chinese	1,479,000	58
Malays	699,000	28
Indians	324,000	13
Others	28,000	1
Total	2,530,000	100

Source: Ooi Jin-Bee, *Peninsular Malaysia*, p. 171.

Appendix 9

RACIAL COMPOSITION OF THE MAJOR TOWNS* OF PENINSULAR MALAYSIA, 1970

Name of Town	Population	Racial Composition (per cent)			
		Malays	Chinese	Indians	Others
1. Kuala Lumpur	452,000	25	55	19	1
2. Georgetown	269,000	14	72	13	1
3. Ipoh	248,000	13	72	14	1
4. Johore Bahru	136,000	50	39	8	3
5. Klang	114,000	21	58	20	1
6. Petaling Jaya	93,000	20	63	14	3
7. Malacca	87,000	15	75	7	3
8. Seremban	81,000	21	59	19	1
9. Alor Star	66,000	40	48	11	1
10. Muar	61,000	37	59	4	—
11. Butterworth	61,000	24	59	16	1
12. Kota Bharu	55,000	68	29	2	1
13. Taiping	55,000	23	58	18	1
14. Kuala Trengganu	53,000	82	16	2	—
15. Batu Pahat	53,000	30	66	4	—
16. Telok Anson	45,000	23	59	18	—
17. Kuantan	43,000	41	49	9	1
18. Kluang	43,000	28	62	10	—
19. Sungei Petani	36,000	28	55	17	—
20. Jinjang	27,000	1	98	1	—
21. Bukit Mertajam	27,000	10	88	12	—
22. Kampar	27,000	9	78	13	—
23. Ayer Hitam	26,000	10	80	10	—
24. Bentong	23,000	15	78	7	—
25. Kajang	22,000	19	67	14	—
26. Sungei Siput North	21,000	10	70	20	—

*'Major towns' are here defined as those with a population of over 20,000.

Source: Ooi Jin-Bee, *Peninsular Malaysia*, p. 164.

Appendix 10

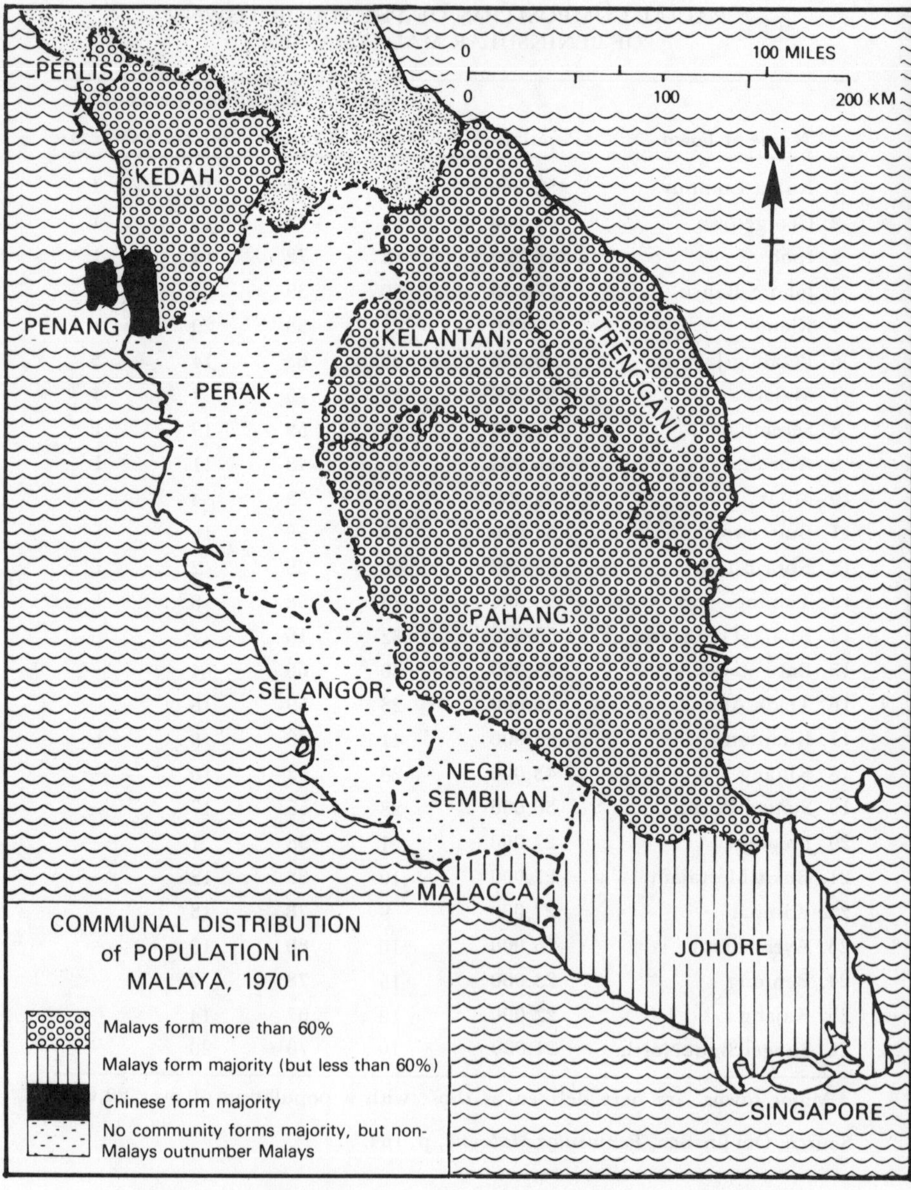

Adapted from Alvin Rabushka, *Race and Politics in Urban Malaya.*

Appendix 11

POPULATION GROWTH IN PENINSULAR MALAYSIA BY ETHNIC GROUPS 1931–1971

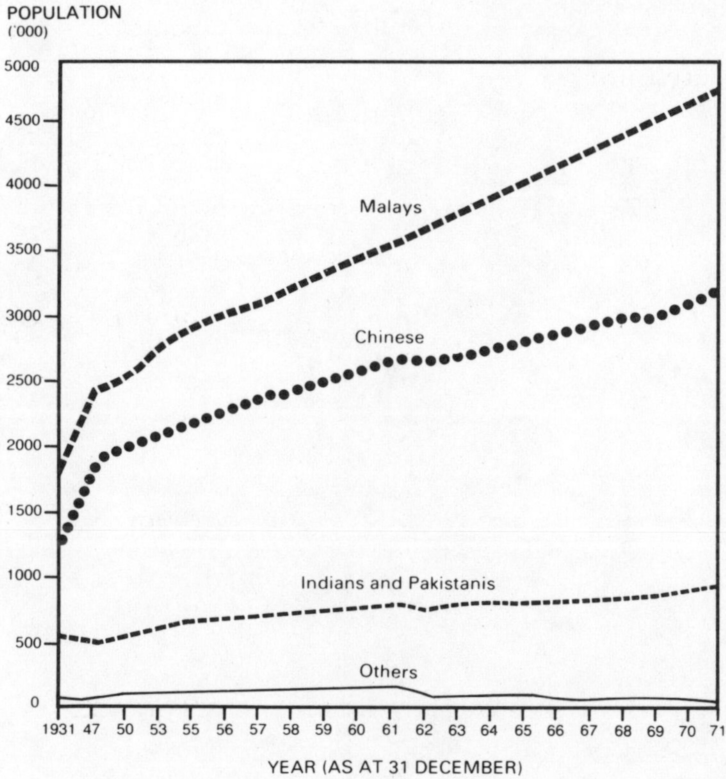

Source: *Malaysia Year Book, 1978.*

Notes

Chapter One

1 Victor Purcell, *The Chinese in Malaya,* Oxford University Press, Kuala Lumpur, 1967, p. 16.

2 N.A. Simoniya, *Overseas Chinese in Southeast Asia — A Russian Study,* Cornell University, Ithaca, New York, 1961, p. 10.

3 cf. Wang Gungwu, *A Short History of the Nanyang Chinese,* pp. 1-12, and the same author's 'The Nanhai Trade: A Study of the Early History of Chinese Trade in the South China Sea', *Journal Malayan Branch Royal Asiatic Society,* Vol. XXXI, Pt. 2, No. 182 (June 1958), pp. 1-135 *passim.*

4 Victor Purcell, *The Chinese in Malaya,* Oxford University Press, Kuala Lumpur, 1967, p. 19.

5 *ibid.*, p. 16

6 Emily Sadka, *The Protected Malay States 1874—1875,* University of Malaya Press, Kuala Lumpur, 1970, pp. 21-22. For a comment on the *babas,* see Purcell, *op. cit.*, pp. 61-2; see, too, Felix Chia, *The Babas,* Times Books International, Singapore, 1980, p. 2.

7 D.K. Bassett, 'The Historical Background, 1500—1815' in Wang Gungwu (ed.) *Malaysia: A Survey,* Pall Mall Press, London, 1964, p. 122.

8 Khoo Kay Kim, *The Western Malay States 1850—1873: The Effects of Commercial Development on Malay Politics,* Oxford University Press, Kuala Lumpur, 1972, pp. 39, 110.

9 N.J. Ryan, *The Making of Modern Malaysia and Singapore,* Oxford University Press, Kuala Lumpur, 1971, p. 123; Khoo, *op. cit.*, pp. 52, 58-9, 69; Wilfred Blythe, *The Impact of Chinese Secret Societies in Malaya,* Oxford University Press, London, 1969, p. 42.

10 Blythe, *op. cit.*, p. 65.

11 Ryan, *op. cit.*, p. 119, quoting a British Government Paper *Correspondence Relating to Native States in the Peninsula:* Parliamentary Papers: C. 1111; Sadka, *op. cit.*, pp. 3-5, 414.

12 Sadka, *op. cit.*, p. 329.

13 W.L. Blythe, 'Historical Sketch of Chinese Labour in Malaya', *Journal Malayan Branch Royal Asiatic Society,* Vol. XX, Pt. 1 (June 1947), pp. 67-8.

14 Rupert Emerson, *Malaysia, A Study in Direct and Indirect Rule,* University of Malaya Press, Kuala Lumpur, 1966 (reprint), p. 29.

15 Joyce Ee, 'Chinese Migration to Singapore, 1896—1941' *Journal of Southeast Asian History,* Vol. 2, No. 1 (March 1961), pp. 48, 50.

16 P.C. Campbell, *Chinese Coolie Emigration to Countries within the British Empire,* P.S. King and Son Ltd., London, 1923, p. xii.

17 Khoo Kay Kim, 'Racial Harmony and Conflict in Southeast Asia: The Example of Malaysia' in *Southeast Asia Today: Problems and Prospects,* Institute of Southeast Asian Studies, Singapore, 1973, p. 11.

18 Blythe, *Historical Sketch of Chinese Labour in Malaya,* pp. 111-13. A good description of a typical *kongsi* (labourers' lines) in a tin mine, written in 1895, is quoted by Blythe although the original source is not stated.

19 In Malaya, all members of the white race are commonly referred to as Europeans.

20 Personal communication with author.

21 Gordon P. Means, *Malaysian Politics*, Hodder and Stoughton, London, 1976 (2nd edn.), p. 17.

22 Emerson, *op. cit.*, p. 478

23 S. Takdir Alisjahbana, *Indonesia: Social and Cultural Revolution,* Oxford University Press, Singapore, 1975 (3rd impression), p. 3.

24 Sir Richard Winstedt, *The Malay Magician being Shaman, Saiva and Sufi,* Routledge and Kegan Paul, London, 1951, pp. 4-6, 39-55; R.D. Hill, *Rice in Malaya: A Study in Historical Geography,* Oxford University Press, Kuala Lumpur, 1977, pp. 42-3; K.M. Endicott, *An Analysis of Malay Magic,* Clarendon Press, Oxford, 1970, pp. 2-4; and S. Husin Ali, *Malay Peasant Society and Leadership,* Oxford University Press, Kuala Lumpur, 1975, pp. 171-3.

25 See Sir Frank Swettenham, *British Malaya,* George Allen and Unwin Ltd., London, 1948 (3rd edn.), pp. 116-17; Richmond L. Wheeler, *The Modern Malay,* George Allen and Unwin Ltd., London, 1928, p. 212; Syed Hussein Alatas, 'Religion and Modernization in South-East Asia', in Hans-Dieter Evers (ed.) *Modernization in South-East Asia,* Oxford University Press, Singapore, 1972, pp. 153-69 *passim;* Hill, *op. cit.*, pp. xvi-xvii.

Chapter Two

1 Before the formation of Malaysia in 1963, the name Malaya was generally used to refer to the Malay states forming the Malay Peninsula, together with the former settlements of Malacca and Penang, and often Singapore was included within the term.
Thereafter, the territories of the Malay Peninsula have been referred to officially as Peninsular Malaysia, although colloquially they are still sometimes called Malaya, while Sabah and Sarawak, which constitute the east wing of Malaysia, are termed East Malaysia.

2 Rupert Emerson, *Malaysia, A Study in Direct and Indirect Rule,* University of Malaya Press, Kuala Lumpur, 1966 (reprint), p. 118; N.J. Ryan, *The Making of Modern Malaysia and Singapore,* Oxford University Press, Kuala Lumpur, 1971, p. 136.

3 Emily Sadka, *The Protected Malay States 1874—1875,* University of Malaya

Press, Kuala Lumpur, 1970 (2nd impression), pp. 47-8; Ryan, *op. cit.*, p. 138; Tan Ding Eing, *A Portrait of Malaysia and Singapore,* Oxford University Press, Singapore, 1975, p. 125; Emerson, *op. cit.*, p. 121.

4 Sir George Maxwell and W.S. Gibson, *Treaties and Engagements Affecting the Malay States and Borneo,* London, 1924, pp. 35-6.

5 Maxwell and Gibson, *op. cit.*, pp. 64-5.

6 Emerson, *op. cit.*, p. 235; Ryan, *op. cit.*, pp. 151-3; Sadka, *op. cit.*, p. 377.

7 Quoted in Emerson, *op. cit.*, p. 139.

8 Emerson, *op. cit.*, pp. 194-268 *passim.*

9 See Pat Barr, *Taming the Jungle: The Men Who Made British Malaya,* Secker and Warburg, London, 1977.

10 Mary F. Somers Heidhues, *Southeast Asia's Chinese Minorities,* Longman Australia Pty. Ltd., 1974.

11 See R.N. Jackson, *Pickering: Protector of Chinese,* Oxford University Press, Kuala Lumpur, 1965; Victor Purcell, *The Chinese in Malaya,* Oxford University Press, London, 1973 (2nd impression), p. 185.

12 *Second Malaysia Plan 1971—5,* Government Press, Kuala Lumpur, 1971; *Third Malaysia Plan 1976—1980,* Government Press, Kuala Lumpur, 1976.

13 Emerson, *op. cit.*, p. 174

14 *ibid.*, pp. 174-5.

15 *ibid.*, p. 175; Ryan, *op. cit.*, p. 191.

16 R.D. Hill, *Rice in Malaya, A Study in Historical Geography,* Oxford University Press, Kuala Lumpur, 1977, p. 120-1, quoting from Resident's Diary, Malacca, 26 August 1828.

17 Emerson, *op. cit.*, pp. 145-6.

18 *ibid.*, p. 153.

19 David McIntyre, 'Political History 1896—1946' in Wang Gungwu (ed.), *Malaysia: A Survey,* Pall Mall Press, London, 1964, p. 142.

20 Tan Cheng Lock, *Malayan Problems: From a Chinese Point of View,* Tannsco, Singapore, 1947, p. 90.

21 *ibid.*, p. 76

22 *ibid.*

23 Emerson, *op. cit.*, p. 173

24 *ibid.*, p. 174; Ryan, *op. cit.*, pp. 192-3; Tan Ding Eing, *op. cit.*, p. 160.

25 Emerson, *op. cit.*, pp. 316-9.

26 Emerson, *op. cit.*, p. 321; Ryan, *op. cit.*, p. 193; Tan Ding Eing, *op. cit.*, p. 160.

27 Emerson, *op. cit.*, pp. 175, 335.

28 Ryan, *op. cit.*, p. 193; Emerson, *op. cit.*, pp. 324-35.

Chapter Three

1 Rupert Emerson, *Malaysia, A Study in Direct and Indirect Rule,* University of Malaya Press, Kuala Lumpur, 1966 (reprint), p. 513, quoting from the Straits Settlements Legislative Council Proceedings, 19 October 1932.

2 The 1931 Census revealed the following breakdown of the population according to major ethnic groups in Malaya (including Singapore):

Malays	1,962,021	(44.7 per cent)
Chinese	1,709,392	(39.0 per cent)
Indians	624,009	(14.2 per cent)

Even more significantly, the percentage increases of the major ethnic groups during the 1911–1921 and 1921–1931 Census periods were as follows:

Ethnic Group	*1911–21*	*1921–31*
Malays	15 per cent	17 per cent
Chinese	28 per cent	46 per cent
Indians	77 per cent	32 per cent

It should be observed that the large influx of Indians during the 1911–21 period was attributable to labourers from India coming to work on the newly-developed rubber estates.

In 1911, the Malays constituted over 53 per cent of the total population but by 1921 they had dropped to just over 49 per cent, and by 1931 they had dropped to under 45 per cent, and this trend continued in spite of a large continuing immigration of Javanese and Sumatrans from the Dutch East Indies.

Another illuminating analysis of the 1931 Census figures, given below, brings out the way in which Malays were vastly outnumbered by non-Malays in the FMS compared with the UMS, and, moreover, it should be borne in mind in this connection, that the main process of development and modernization was taking place in the west and not in the east coast states of the Malay Peninsula:

Territory	*Malays*	*% of Total Population*	*Chinese & Indians*	*% of Total Population*
FMS	593,731	34.7	1,091,536	63.7
UMS	1,055,853	69.2	441,808	28.9

3 Emerson, *op. cit.*, p. 195.

4 Joyce Ee, 'Chinese Migration to Singapore, 1896–1941', *Journal of Southeast Asian History,* Vol. 2, No. 1 (March 1961), p. 51.

5 Emerson, *op. cit.*, p. 278; N.J. Ryan, *The Making of Modern Malaysia and Singapore,* Oxford University Press, Kuala Lumpur, 1971, p. 209.

[6] Ee, *op. cit.*, p. 43.

[7] Ryan, *op. cit.*, pp. 208-9; R.S. Milne and Diane K. Mauzy, *Politics and Government in Malaysia,* Federal Publications, Singapore, 1978, pp. 24-5.

[8] Ryan, *op. cit.*, P. 201; Emerson, *op. cit.*, pp. 182, 185; J.M. Gullick, *Malaysia,* Ernest Benn Ltd., London, 1969, p. 75; Rex Stevenson, *Cultivators and Administrators, British Educational Policy towards the Malays 1875—1906,* Oxford University Press, Kuala Lumpur, 1975, p.6.

[9] Emerson, *op. cit.*, p. 514.

[10] Tan Cheng Lock, *Malayan Problems: From a Chinese Point of View,* Tannsco, Singapore, 1947, p. 27; C.M. Turnbull, 'British Planning for Post-war Malaysia', *Journal of Southeast Asian Studies,* Vol. 5, No. 2, (September 1974), p. 241.

[11] K.J. Ratnam, *Communalism and the Political Process in Malaya,* University of Malaya Press, Kuala Lumpur, 1967 (reprint), pp. 105-6.

[12] Stevenson, *op. cit.*, p. 181.

[13] Paul Chang, *Planning Education for a Plural Society,* International Institute for Educational Planning, UNESCO, Paris, 1971, p. 27; Milne and Mauzy, *op. cit.*, p. 26.

[14] Victor Purcell, *The Chinese in Southeast Asia,* Oxford University Press, London, 1965 (2nd edn.), p. 278; Tan Cheng Lock, *op. cit.*, pp. 95-110.

[15] Chang, *op. cit.*, p. 10

[16] Emerson, *op. cit.*, p. 517.

[17] Emerson, *op. cit.*, pp. 478-9; *The Economic Development of Malaya, Report of a Mission organized by the International Bank for Reconstruction and Development,* Government Printer, Singapore, 1955, p. 227.

[18] *The Economic Development of Malaya, op. cit.*, pp. 57-61; R.D. Hill, *Rice in Malaya, A Study in Historical Geography,* Oxford University Press, Kuala Lumpur, 1977, pp. 45-6, 80-1, 88-90, 112, 119, 122-5, 136-7, 196.

[19] Emerson, *op. cit.*, p. 479.

[20] *ibid.*

[21] *The Economic Development of Malaya, op. cit.*, p. 227.

Chapter Four

[1] Rupert Emerson, *Malaysia, A Study in Direct and Indirect Rule,* University of Malaya Press, Kuala Lumpur, 1966 (reprint), pp. 54, 282, 297, 509.

[2] Emerson, *op. cit.*, p. 511; N.J. Ryan, *The Making of Modern Malaysia and Singapore,* Oxford University Press, Kuala Lumpur, 1971, p. 214.

[3] J.M. Gullick, *Malaysia,* Ernest Benn Ltd., London, 1969, p. 88.

[4] Tan Cheng Lock, *Malayan Problems: From a Chinese Point of View,* Tannsco, Singapore, 1947, pp. 72, 79; Emerson, *op. cit.*, p. 54; C.M. Turnbull,

'British Planning for Post-war Malaysia', *Journal of Southeast Asian Studies,* Vol. 5, No. 2, September 1974, p. 240.

5 Yoichi Itagaki, 'Some Aspects of the Japanese Policy for Malaya under the Occupation, with special reference to Nationalism' in K.G. Tregonning (ed.), *Papers on Malayan History,* University of Malaya in Singapore, 1962, p. 256.

6 C.M. Turnbull, *A History of Singapore 1819—1975,* Oxford University Press, Kuala Lumpur, 1977, p. 188.

7 Joyce C. Lebra, *Japanese-Trained Armies in Southeast Asia,* Heinemann Educational Books (Asia) Ltd., Hong Kong, 1977, p. 113; Itagaki, *op. cit.*, pp. 262-4.

8 Lebra, *op. cit.*, p. 75.

9 Gordon P. Means, *Malaysian Politics,* Hodder & Stoughton, London, 1976 (2nd edn.), p. 45; R.S. Milne and Diane K. Mauzy, *Politics and Government in Malaysia,* Federal Publications, Singapore, 1978, p. 22.

10 David McIntyre, 'Political History 1896—1946' in Wang Gungwu (ed.), *Malaysia: A Survey,* Pall Mall Press, London, 1964, p. 146; Itagaki, *op. cit.*, pp. 263, 266.

11 Lebra, *op. cit.*, p. 120; Itagaki, *op. cit.*, p. 263; Gullick, *op. cit.*, p. 95; Ryan, *op. cit.*, p. 213.

12 Lebra, *op. cit.*, p. 121; Tan Ding Eing, *A Portrait of Malaysia and Singapore,* Oxford University Press, Singapore, 1975, p. 211; Nicholas Tarling, *Sukarno and Indonesian Unity,* Heinemann Educational Books, Auckland, 1977, p. 15; Malcolm Caldwell, *Indonesia,* Oxford University Press, London, 1968, pp. 78-9.

13 Tarling, *op. cit.*, p. 15

14 Lebra, *op. cit.*, p. 121; Itagaki, *op. cit.*, pp. 264-5.
Ibrahim Ya'acob continued to live in Jakarta until he died in 1980.

15 Milne and Mauzy, *op. cit.*, p. 22.

16 Norton Ginsburg and Chester F. Roberts, Jnr. (eds.), *Malaya,* University of Washington Press, Seattle, 1958, pp. 460, 462.

17 Ryan, *op. cit.*, pp. 227-8; Itagaki, *op. cit.*, p. 256; Gullick, *op. cit.*, p. 100.

18 Tan Cheng Lock, *op. cit.*, p. 46.

19 C.M. Turnbull, 'British Planning for Post-war Malaysia', *op. cit.*, pp. 245-6; Tan Cheng Lock, *op. cit.*, pp. 4-5.

20 Tan Cheng Lock, *op. cit.*, p. 5.

21 *ibid.*, p. 17.

22 *ibid.*, pp. 32, 10-42.

23 C.M. Turnbull, 'British Planning for Post-war Malaysia', *op. cit.*, pp. 245-6.

24 Mohamed Noordin Sopiee, *From Malayan Union to Singapore Separation. Political Unification in the Malaysian Region, 1945—65,* University of Malaya

Press, 1974, p. 12, 16; Ryan, *op. cit.*, pp. 289 ff; Lennox A. Mills, *British Rule in Eastern Asia,* The University of Minnesota Press, Minneapolis, 1942, pp. 33-42; Means, *op. cit.*, pp. 51-3; C.M. Turnbull, 'British Planning for Post-war Malaysia', *op. cit.*, p. 243.

25 K.J. Ratnam, *Communalism and the Political Process in Malaya,* University of Malaya Press, Kuala Lumpur, 1967 (reprint), p. 75.

26 Sopiee, *op. cit.*, pp. 24, 29; Ryan, *op. cit.*, p. 228.

27 Milne and Mauzy, *op. cit.*, p. 28.

28 Means, *op. cit.*, p. 53; Yeo Kim Wah, *Political Development in Singapore 1945—55,* Singapore University Press, 1973, pp. 17-18; Sopiee, *op. cit.*, p. 25.

29 Tan Cheng Lock, *op. cit.*, p. 71.

30 Yeo, *op. cit.*, p. 19; Ryan, *op. cit.*, p. 231; Sopiee, *op. cit.*, p. 37; Milne, *op. cit.*, pp. 38-9, 42.

31 Ratnam, *op. cit.*, p. 105, quoting the Federation of Malaya Agreement, 1948, Clause 19 (i) (d); Milne and Mauzy, *op. cit.*, pp. 29-31.

32 Means, *op. cit.*, p. 56.

33 Yeo, *op. cit.*, p. 32. See also Ryan, *op. cit.*, p. 231; Ratnam, *op. cit.*, p. 104; Means, *op. cit.*, pp. 55-9.

34 Yeo, *op. cit.*, pp. 32-3; Ryan, *op. cit.*, pp. 231-2; Nam Tae Yul, *Racism, Nationalism and Nation-Building in Malaysia and Singapore (A Functional Analysis of Political Integration),* Sadha Prakashan, Meerut, India, 1973, pp. 20-4.

35 Ratnam, *op. cit.*, p. 84.

36 Means, *op. cit.*, p. 114.

Chapter Five

1 Gordon Means, *Malaysian Politics,* Hodder and Stoughton, London, 1976 (2nd edn.), p. 78; John W. Henderson, *Area Handbook for Malaysia,* American University, Washington, D.C., 1970, p. 60; Edgar O'Ballance, *Malaya: The Communist Insurgent War, 1948—1960,* Faber and Faber Ltd., London, 1966, p. 89.

2 Gene Z. Hanrahan, *The Communist Struggle in Malaya,* University of Malaya Press, Kuala Lumpur, 1971, p. 108; Lennox A. Mills, *British Malaya, 1824—67,* Oxford University Press, Kuala Lumpur, 1966 (reprint), p. 44 *passim.*

3 Means, *op. cit.*, p. 76; *The Federation of Malaya and Its Police 1786—1952,* Government Printer, Kuala Lumpur, 1952, p. 28; N.J. Ryan, *The Making of Modern Malaysia and Singapore,* Oxford University Press, Kuala Lumpur, 1971, p. 236.

4 *The Federation of Malaya and Its Police, op. cit.*, p. 31; Hanrahan, *op. cit.*, p. 109.

5 Mills, *op. cit.*, p. 51; *The Federation of Malaya and Its Police, op. cit.*, p. 32.

6 *The Federation of Malaya and Its Police, op. cit.*, p. 31.

7 Means, *op. cit.*, p. 18; *The Federation of Malaya and Its Police, op. cit.*, pp. 31, 33.

8 *The Federation of Malaya and Its Police, op. cit.*, pp. 33, 38; Mills, *op. cit.*, pp. 51, 55 *passim.*

9 Ryan, *op. cit.*, pp. 238-9; Mills, *op. cit.*, p. 56; *The Federation of Malaya and Its Police, op. cit.*, pp. 33-4; Hanrahan, *op. cit.*, pp. 140-2; Virginia Thompson and Richard Adloff, *Minority Problems in Southeast Asia*, Stanford University Press, Stanford, California, 1955, pp. 34-5.

10 Anthony Short, *The Communist Insurrection in Malaya 1948—1960*, Frederick Muller Ltd., London, 1975, p. 401.

11 Thompson, *op. cit.*, p. 35.

12 Mills, *op. cit.*, p. 55.

13 *ibid.*

14 *ibid.*, p. 54.

15 Short, *op. cit.*, pp. 301-2, 314.

16 Thompson, *op. cit.*, p. 33.

17 Short, *op. cit.*, pp. 301-2.

18 Thompson, *op. cit.*, p. 36.

19 R.S. Milne, *Malaya: A Political and Economic Appraisal,* Greenwood Press Publisher, Westport, Connecticut, 1973 (reprint), p. 34; K.J. Ratnam, *Communalism and the Political Process in Malaya,* University of Malaya Press, Kuala Lumpur, 1967 (reprint), p. 20; W.R. Roff, *The Origins of Malay Nationalism,* University of Malaya Press, Kuala Lumpur, 1967, pp. 41-2; Short, *op. cit.*, p. 265.

Sir Henry Gurney told the writer, who was Sir Henry's Hon. Aide-de-Camp in May 1949, that he had put up the idea of forming a Chinese association along the same lines as UMNO to Ong Shook Lin, Colonel Sir Henry Hau-sik Lee and Leong Yew Koh.

20 Mills, *op. cit.*, quoting *The Straits Times,* 12 December 1948.

21 *ibid,* pp. 72-3; R.S. Milne and Diane K. Mauzy, *Politics and Government in Malaysia,* Federal Publications, Singapore, 1978, pp. 34-5; Ryan, *op. cit.*, p. 245.

22 Mills, *op. cit.*, pp. 75-6; Francis Wong Hoi Kee and Ee Tiang Hong, *Education in Malaysia,* Heinemann Educational Books (Asia) Ltd., Hong Kong, 1971, pp. 52-3.

23 Wong, *op. cit.*, pp. 54-5; Roff, *op. cit.*, p. 49.

24 Mills, *op. cit.*, pp. 75-6.

25 Wong, *op. cit.*, p. 56.

[26] Leon Comber, 'Chinese Education — A Perennial Malayan Problem', *Asian Survey,* Vol. 1, No. 8 (October 1961), p. 33.

[27] Comber, *op. cit.*, p. 34.

[28] William Shaw, *Tun Razak — His Life and Times,* Longman Malaysia Sdn. Bhd., Kuala Lumpur, 1976, p. 92.

[29] Means, *op. cit.*, p. 122.

[30] *ibid.*, pp. 123-5; Mills, *op. cit.*, pp. 75-6; Thompson, *op. cit.*, pp. 35-7; Milne and Mauzy, *op. cit.*, p. 126.

[31] Milne and Mauzy, *op. cit.*, p. 126-7; Means, *op. cit.*, p. 122.

[32] Mills, *op. cit.*, pp. 78-9; Milne and Mauzy, *op. cit.*, pp. 126-9; Means, *op. cit.*, pp. 126-37.

[33] Roff, *op. cit.*, p. 43; Mills, *op. cit.*, p. 80; Milne and Mauzy, *op. cit.*, pp. 126-9; Thompson, *op. cit.*, p. 37.

[34] Milne and Mauzy, *op. cit.*, p. 36; Thompson, *op. cit.*, p. 38.

[35] Means, *op. cit.*, p. 169n.

[36] Milne and Mauzy, *op. cit.*, pp. 36-7; Means, *op. cit.*, pp. 170-92; Thompson, *op. cit.*, pp. 96-7; Ryan, *op. cit.*, p. 247.

[37] Means, *op. cit.*, p. 172.

[38] Tunku Abdul Rahman Putra Al-Haj, *Looking Back. Monday Musings and Memories,* Pustaka Antara, Kuala Lumpur, 1977, pp. 59, 178; Thompson, *op. cit.*, p. 102; Milne and Mauzy, *op. cit.*, p. 39.

[39] Means, *op. cit.*, pp. 198-9; Milne and Mauzy, *op. cit.*, p. 36.

[40] Milne, *op. cit.*, pp. 174-5.

[41] Milne and Mauzy, *op. cit.*, p. 60.

[42] Means, *op. cit.*, pp. 175-89; Milne and Mauzy, *op. cit.*, pp. 38-42; Ratnam, *op. cit.*, pp. 109-141.

[43] Milne and Mauzy, *op. cit.*, p. 48.
In 1958, 800,000 non-Malays became citizens.

[44] Ratnam, *op. cit.*, p. 106.

[45] *ibid.*

[46] Milne and Mauzy, *op. cit.*, p. 40

[47] Means, *op. cit.*, p. 179.

[48] Milne and Mauzy, *op. cit.*, p. 39.

[49] Tunku Abdul Rahman, *op. cit.*, pp. 70-1.

Chapter Six

[1] Mohamed Noordin Sopiee, *From Malayan Union to Singapore Separation. Political Unification in the Malaysian Region 1945—65,* University of Malaya Press, Kuala Lumpur, 1974, pp. 125, 127-8; Tunku Abdul Rahman Putra Al-Haj, *Looking Back. Monday Musings and Memories,* Pustaka Antara, Kuala Lumpur, 1977, p.81.

[2] R.S. Milne and Diane K. Mauzy, *Politics and Government in Malaysia,* Federal Publications, Singapore, 1978, p. 55.

[3] Sopiee, *op. cit.*, p. 133.

[4] *ibid.*, pp. 125-7.

[5] *ibid.*, p. 57.

[6] Milne and Mauzy, *op. cit.*, p. 69.

[7] Mat Salleh (pseud. Leon Comber), 'Malays and Chinese Brothers?', *Eastern World,* London, August 1962, p. 20.

[8] *ibid.*

[9] Milne and Mauzy, *op. cit.*, pp. 62-3.

[10] C.M. Turnbull, *A History of Singapore 1819—1975,* Oxford University Press, Kuala Lumpur, 1977, p. 281.

[11] Milne and Mauzy, *op. cit.*, pp. 321-2.

[12] *ibid.*, pp. 322-3; Gordon P. Means, *Malaysian Politics,* Hodder and Stoughton, London, 1976 (2nd edn.), p. 16; *Malaysia Year Book, 1970,* The Malay Mail, Kuala Lumpur (n.d.), p. 72.

[13] *Second Malaysia Plan 1971—5,* Government Press, Kuala Lumpur, 1971, p. 15.

[14] Milne and Mauzy, *op. cit.*, p. 323; Means, *op. cit.*, p. 16; *Malaysia Year Book, 1970, op. cit.*, p. 93.

For the example of *padi kunca* referred to see S. Husin Ali, *Malay Peasant Society and Leadership,* Oxford University Press, Kuala Lumpur, 1975, pp. 81-2.

[15] Victor Purcell, *The Chinese in Southeast Asia,* Oxford University Press, London, 1965 (2nd edn.), p. 286.

[16] *Second Malaysia Plan 1971—5, op. cit.*, p. 13.

[17] Ooi Jin-Bee, *Peninsular Malaysia,* Longman, London, 1976, p. 171.

[18] *Second Malaysia Plan 1971—5, op. cit.*, p. 18.

[19] *ibid.*, pp. 1-48 *passim.* See also J.M. Gullick, *Malaysia,* Ernest Benn Ltd., London, 1969, pp. 221-241.

[20] Ooi, *op. cit.*, p. 171.

[21] *Second Malaysia Plan 1971—5, op. cit.*, pp. 39-40.

[22] *ibid.*, p. 41.

[23] Sopiee, *op. cit.*, p. 186.

[24] Chan Heng Chee, *Singapore, The Politics of Survival 1965—1967,* Oxford University Press, Singapore, 1971, pp. 8, 10; Nancy McHenry Fletcher, *The Separation of Singapore from Malaysia,* Cornell University, Ithaca, New York, 1969, p. 33. See also Turnbull, *op. cit.*, pp. 287-93.

[25] Chan, *op. cit.*, p. 9; Sopiee, *op. cit.*, pp. 185-9.

[26] Chan, *op. cit.*, p. 6.

[27] Gullick, *op. cit.*, p. 179.

[28] Fletcher, *op. cit.*, p. 248; Sopiee, *op. cit.*, p. 193.

[29] Gullick, *op. cit.*, pp. 179-80.

[30] Fletcher, *op. cit.*, p. 59.

[31] *ibid.*, p. 40.

[32] Fletcher, *op. cit.*, p. 37; Sopiee, *op. cit.*, p. 194.

[33] Means, *op. cit.*, p. 343; Fletcher, *op. cit.*, p. 37.

[34] Turnbull, *op. cit.*, p. 291.

[35] Fletcher, *op. cit.*, p. 42.

[36] *ibid.;* Turnbull, *op. cit.*, p. 43.

[37] Fletcher, *op. cit.*, p. 44.

[38] Turnbull, *op. cit.*, p. 291, quoting from *Information for 1949 transmitted to the United Nations* (Singapore 1949).

[39] Lee Kuan Yew, *The Battle for a Malaysian Malaysia,* Government Printing Office, Singapore, 1965, p. 39. Dato Abdul Razak's comment is taken from Fletcher, *op. cit.*, quoting *The Straits Times,* 11 May 1965.

[40] Fletcher, *op. cit.*, pp. 62-3.

[41] Rahman, *op. cit.*, p. 127.

[42] Milne and Mauzy, *op. cit.*, p. 74.

[43] *ibid.*, p. 74, quoting *The Straits Times,* 4 July 1969; Sopiee, *op. cit.*, p. 180.

[44] Means, *op. cit.*, p. 356; R.K. Vasil, *The Malaysian General Election of 1969,* Oxford University Press, Singapore, 1972, pp. 14-7.

[45] Milne and Mauzy, *op. cit.*, pp. 67-73.

[46] Vasil, *op. cit.*, p. 14, K.J. Ratnam, *Communalism and the Political Process in Malaya,* University of Malaya Press, Kuala Lumpur, 1967 (reprint), p. 140.

[47] Means, *op. cit.*, p. 391; Gullick, *op. cit.*, pp. 267-73.

[48] Milne and Mauzy, *op. cit.*, p. 368; Gullick, *op. cit.*, p. 270; Means, *op. cit.*, p. 392.

[49] Tunku Abdul Rahman Putra Al-Haj, *Viewpoints,* Heinemann Educational Books (Asia) Ltd., Kuala Lumpur, 1978, pp. 198 *et seq.*

[50] Means, *op. cit.*, p. 392.

Chapter Seven

1 Goh Cheng Teik, *The May 13th Incident and Democracy in Malaysia,* Oxford University Press, Kuala Lumpur, 1971, p. 24.

2 Lau Teik Soon, 'Malaysia: The May 13 Incident', *Australia's Neighbours,* July-Aug, 1969; quoted by N.J. Funston, *Malay Politics in Malaysia. A Study of UMNO and PAS,* Heinemann Educational Books (Asia) Ltd., Kuala Lumpur, 1980, p. 208.

3 *The May 13 Tragedy, A Report,* The National Operations Council, Kuala Lumpur, 1969, p. 21; Tunku Abdul Rahman Putra Al-Haj, *May 13 Before and After,* Utusan Melayu Press Ltd., Kuala Lumpur, 1969, p.17.

4 R.K. Vasil, *The Malaysian General Election of 1969,* Oxford University Press, Singapore, 1972, pp. 56-9.

5 *The Straits Times,* 9 May 1969.

6 Rahman, *op. cit.*, p. 28.

7 R.S. Milne and Diane K. Mauzy, *Politics and Government in Malaysia,* Federal Publications, Singapore, 1978, p. 143; Vasil, *op. cit.*, p. 21.

8 Vasil, *op. cit.*, pp. 27-8.

9 *Who Lives if Malaysia Dies?,* Democratic Action Party, Petaling Jaya, Selangor, Malaysia, 1969, pp. iv-vi, 20-1.

10 Vasil, *op. cit.*, pp. 29-30.

11 Goh, *op. cit.*, p. 47.

12 *ibid.;* Milne and Mauzy, *op. cit.*, p. 150.

13 Goh, *op. cit.*, p. 57.

14 Rahman, *op. cit.*, p. 45.

15 *ibid.*, pp. 46-62.

16 *The May 13 Tragedy, op. cit.*, p. 28.

17 Vasil, *op. cit.*, p. 17, 63-5.

18 See Syed Hussein Alatas, *The Sociology of Corruption,* Donald Moore Press Ltd., Singapore, 1968.

19 Vasil, *op. cit.*, pp. 63-5.

20 K.J. Ratnam and R.S. Milne, 'The 1969 Parliamentary Election in West Malaysia', *Pacific Affairs,* Vol. XLIII, No. 2., Summer 1970, pp. 215-6; Vasil, *op. cit.*, p. 65; Milne and Mauzy, *op. cit.*, p. 149.

21 Goh, *op. cit.*, p. 13; Stuart Drummond and David Hawkins, 'The Malaysian Elections of 1969: Analysis of the Campaign and the Results', *Asian Survey,* Vol. 10, No. 4 (April 1970), pp. 331-3.

22 Goh, *op. cit.*, pp. 12-13.

23 *The Straits Times,* 11 May 1969.

24 Rahman, *op. cit.*, p. 64.

25 Vasil, *op. cit.*, p. 37; Milne and Mauzy, *op. cit.*, p. 164.

26 Goh, *op. cit.*, pp. 16-17.

27 Rahman, *op. cit.*, p. 76.

28 Goh, *op. cit.*, p. 21; Rahman, *op. cit.*, pp. 75-8; *The May 13 Tragedy, op. cit.*, p. 32.

29 Rahman, *op. cit.*, pp. 93-4.

30 See Tunku Abdul Rahman Putra Al-Haj, *May 13 Before and After*, Utusan Melayu Press Ltd., Kuala Lumpur, 1969; *The May 13 Tragedy, A Report*, The National Operations Council, Kuala Lumpur, 1969; John Slimming, *Malaysia, Death of a Democracy*, John Murray, London, 1969; Felix V. Gagliano, *Communal Violence in Malaysia 1969: the Political Aftermath*, Ohio University Center for International Studies, 1970.

31 *The May 13 Tragedy, op. cit.*, pp. 87-93.

32 *The Straits Times*, 9 May 1969; Rahman, *op. cit.*, p. 177.

33 Jerome R. Bass, 'Malaysia: Continuity or Change?', *Asian Survey*, Vol. 10, no. 2, February 1970, p. 1521; Rahman, *op. cit.*, p. 9; *The May 13 Tragedy, op. cit.*, pp. 15-20; *The Straits Times*, 15 May 1969.

34 *The Straits Times*, 17 May 1969.

35 *The Straits Times*, 20 May 1969.

36 Milne and Mauzy, *op. cit.*, p. 81.

37 *The May 13 Tragedy, op. cit.*, p. 15.

38 *The May 13 Tragedy, op. cit.*, pp. 15-20; Gagliano, *op. cit.*, pp. 7-10.

Chapter Eight

1 Tunku Abdul Rahman Putra Al-Haj, *May 13 Before and After*, Utusan Melayu Press Ltd., Kuala Lumpur, 1969, pp. 8-14, 22-8.

2 Felix V. Gagliano, *Communal Violence in Malaysia 1969: the Political Aftermath*, Ohio University Center for International Studies, 1970, p. 23; *The Straits Times*, 21 June 1969.

3 *The Straits Times*, 19 May 1969.

4 *ibid.*, 14 June 1969; *ibid.*, 2 July 1969; *The May 13 Tragedy, A Report*, The National Operations Council, Kuala Lumpur, 1969, pp. 25-6.

5 *ibid.*, p. ix.

6 *ibid.*

7 Letter by 'Kampong Malay' in the correspondence column of *The Straits Times*, 7 July 1951.

8 Gordon P. Means, *Malaysian Politics*, Hodder and Stoughton, London, 1976 (2nd edn.), p. 408.

9 R.S. Milne and Diane K. Mauzy, *Politics and Government in Malaysia,* Federal Publications, Singapore, 1978, p. 85.

10 See *Keesing's Contemporary Archives,* 1969, pp. 22413-4.

11 Rahman, *op. cit.*, p. 136.

12 *The Straits Times,* 12 June 1969.

13 Means, *op. cit.*, p. 400.

14 Milne and Mauzy, *op. cit.*, p. 88; *Second Malaysia Plan 1971—1975,* Government Press, Kuala Lumpur, 1971, p. 236.

15 See *Far Eastern Economic Review,* Vol. 100, No. 25, 23 June 1978, pp. 14-16, for comments by the Malaysian Minister of Education (Datuk Musa Hitam) on the reasons for the choice of Bahasa Malaysia as the sole medium of instruction in the educational system.

16 Rahman, *op. cit.*, p. 117.

17 Goh Cheng Teik, *The May Thirteenth Incident and Democracy in Malaysia,* Oxford University Press, Kuala Lumpur, 1971, p. 29-30; Gagliano, *op. cit.*, p. 28; Means, *op. cit.*, p. 298; William Shaw, *Tun Razak — His Life and Times,* Longman Malaysia Sdn. Bhd., Kuala Lumpur, 1976, p. 215.

18 Milne and Mauzy, *op. cit.*, p. 87.

The first prime minister of Malaysia was YTM Tunku Abdul Rahman Putra Al-Haj (1963—70); when he resigned, he was succeeded by Tun Abdul Razak (1970—76). After Tun Razak's death in 1976, Datuk Hussein Onn assumed office, and on Datuk Hussein Onn's resignation on account of ill-health in 1981, he was succeeded by Datuk Seri Dr. Mahathir Mohamad.

19 Rahman, *op. cit.*, pp. 117-43.

20 Gagliano, *op. cit.*, pp. 19-20, Means, *op. cit.*, p. 399.

21 *The Straits Times,* 7 August 1969.

22 The Tunku told the writer on 27 December 1977 in Penang that the Malay Brigade in Kedah (the Tunku's home state) took an oath of allegiance to him, and similar oaths were taken by the armed forces and police throughout the country.

23 Milne and Mauzy, *op. cit.*, p. 89.

24 Means, *op. cit.*, pp. 400-1; Shaw, *op. cit.*, p. 216.

25 *The May 13 Tragedy, op. cit.*, p. vi.

26 Means, *op. cit.*, p. 400.

27 *The May 13 Tragedy, op. cit.*, p. 86.

28 Means, *op. cit.*, p. 400; Milne and Mauzy, *op. cit.*, pp. 91-3.

29 Means, *op. cit.*, p. 414; Milne and Mauzy, *op. cit.*, p. 93n.

30 Niels Mulder, *Mysticism and Everyday Life in Contemporary Java, Cultural Persistence and Change,* Singapore University Press, 1978, p. 39, quoting T. Iskandar; *Kamus Dewan,* Dewan Bahasa dan Pustaka, Kuala Lumpur, 1970, p. 981.

31 Means, *op. cit.*, pp. 401-2.

32 Means, *op. cit.*, p. 402, Shaw, *op. cit.*, pp. 219-20.

33 Means, *op. cit.*, p. 402.

34 Shaw, *op. cit.*, pp. 220-1.

35 Milne and Mauzy, *op. cit.*, pp. 97-9; Means, *op. cit.*, p. 403.

36 Milne and Mauzy, *op. cit.*, p. 324.

37 *Second Malaysia Plan 1971—1975, op. cit.*, p. 1.

38 *Mid-Term Review of the Second Malaysia Plan 1971—1975,* Government Press, Kuala Lumpur, 1973, p. 96.

39 Basil J. Moore, *Restructuring Wealth Ownership,* Universiti Sains Malaysia, Pulau Pinang, 1975, pp. 11-25.

40 Means, *op. cit.*, p. 409.

41 *Mid-Term Review of the Second Malaysia Plan 1971—1975, op. cit.*, p. 141.

42 *Second Malaysia Plan 1971—1975, op. cit.*, pp. 41-5; Milne and Mauzy, *op. cit.*, p. 331; Means, *op. cit.*, p. 410.

43 *The Straits Times,* 11 January 1972.

44 *Second Malaysia Plan 1971—1975, op. cit.*, pp. 158-61; Milne and Mauzy, *op. cit.*, p. 334.

45 *ibid.*, p. 335.

46 *Second Malaysia Plan 1971—1975, op. cit.*, p. 1.

47 *ibid.*, pp. 225-6.

48 *Malaysia Year Book 1973/74,* The Malay Mail, Kuala Lumpur, 1974, p. 178.

49 *Second Malaysia Plan 1971—1975, op. cit.*, p. 1.

50 Tun Abdul Razak's view was '.... the government policy on national unity is not by process of assimilation but by integration, that is, by mutual adjustment of diverse cultural and social traits, acceptable to all races in the country'. See Milne and Mauzy, *op. cit.*, p. 366, quoting from *The Straits Times,* 16 May 1972.

51 *Second Malaysia Plan 1971—1975, op. cit.*, pp. v-vi.

52 Milne and Mauzy, *op. cit.*, p. 371; Tjoa Hock Guan, 'Chinese Malaysians and Malaysian Politics, in *Southeast Asian Affairs 1978,* Institute of Southeast Asian Studies/Heinemann Educational Books (Asia) Ltd., Singapore, 1978, p. 189.

Bibliography

Abdul Rahman Putra Al-Haj, Tunku, *May 13 Before and After*, Utusan Melayu Press Ltd., Kuala Lumpur, 1969.

— *Looking Back. Monday Musings and Memories*, Pustaka Antara, Kuala Lumpur, 1977.

— *Viewpoints*, Heinemann Educational Books (Asia) Ltd., Kuala Lumpur, 1978.

Akashi, Y., 'Japanese Policy towards the Malayan Chinese, 1941—45', *Journal of Southeast Asian Studies*, Vol. 1, No. 2 (1970), pp. 61-89.

Alatas, Syed Hussein, 'Religion and Modernization in South-East Asia', in Evers, Han-Dieter (ed.). *Modernization in South-East Asia*, Oxford University Press, Singapore, 1973, pp. 153-69.

— *The Second Malaysia Plan 1971—1975; A Critique*, Institute of Southeast Asian Studies, Singapore, 1974 (reprint).

Alexander, Garth, *Silent Invasion: the Chinese in SE Asia*, Macdonald, London, 1973.

Alisjahbana, S. Takdir, *Indonesia: Social and Cultural Revolution*, Oxford University Press, Singapore, 1975 (3rd impression).

Amyot, Jacques, *The Chinese and the National Integration in Southeast Asia*, Institute of Asian Studies, Faculty of Political Science, Chulalongkorn University, Bangkok, 1972.

Barr, Pat, *Taming of the Jungle: The Men Who Made British Malaya*, Secker and Warburg, London, 1977.

Bass, Jerome R., 'Malaysia: Continuity or Change?', *Asian Survey*, Vol. 10, No. 2, February 1970, pp. 152-60.

— *Malaysian Politics, 1960—1970: Crisis and Response*, Ann Arbor, Michigan, University Microfilms International, 1977.

Bassett, D.K., 'The Historical Background, 1500—1815', in Wang Gungwu (ed.) *Malaysia: A Survey*, Pall Mall Press, London, 1964.

Blythe, W.L., 'Historical Sketch of Chinese Labour in Malaya', *Malayan Branch Royal Asiatic Society*, Vol. XX, Pt.1 (June 1947), pp. 64-114.

— *The Impact of Chinese Secret Societies in Malaya*, Oxford University Press, London, 1969.

Boyce, Peter, 'Policy Without Authority: Singapore's External Affairs Power', *Journal of Southeast Asian History*, Vol. VI, No. 2 (September 1965), pp. 87-103.

Caldwell, Malcolm, *Indonesia*, Oxford University Press, London, 1968.

Campbell, Persia Crawford, *Chinese Coolie Emigration to Countries within the British Empire,* P.S. King and Son Ltd., London, 1923.

Carlson, Sevine, *Malaysia: Search for National Unity and Economic Growth,* Sage Publications, Beverley Hills, California, 1975.

Chai Hon Chan,. *The Development of British Malaya, 1876—1909,* Oxford University Press, Kuala Lumpur, 1964.

Chan Heng Chee, *Singapore, The Politics of Survival 1965—1967,* Oxford University Press, Singapore, 1971.

Chang, Paul, *Planning Education for a Plural Society,* International Institute for Educational Planning, UNESCO, Paris, 1971.

Chee, Stephen, 'Malaysia and Singapore: Separate Identities, Different Priorities', *Asian Survey,* February 1973, pp. 151-61.

Cheng U Wen, 'Opium in the Straits Settlements', *Journal of Southeast Asian History,* Vol. 2, No. 1 (March 1961), pp. 52-75.

Chew, E., 'British Intervention in Malaya. A Reconsideration', *Journal of Southeast Asian History,* Vol. 6, No. 1 (March 1965), pp. 81-93.

Chia, Felix, *The Babas,* Times Books International, Singapore, 1980.

Comber, Leon, 'Chinese Secret Societies in Malaya: an Introduction', *Journal Malayan Branch Royal Asiatic Society,* Vol. XXIX, Pt. 1 (May 1956), pp. 146-62.

— 'Chinese Secret Societies and Merdeka', *Eastern World,* London, August, 1957.

— 'Chinese Secret Societies in Malaya' in Ginsburg, Norton and Roberts, Chester F., Jnr., *Malaya,* University of Washington Press, Seattle, 1958, pp. 282-95.

— 'Chinese Education — A Perennial Malayan Problem', *Asian Survey,* Vol. I, No. 8 (October, 1961), pp. 30-5.

— See Mat Salleh, (pseud. Comber, Leon), 'Malays and Chinese Brothers?', *Eastern World,* London, August 1962, p. 20.

Dahlan, H. (ed.), *The Nescent (sic) Malaysian Society: Development, Trends and Problems,* Jabatan Kebangsaan dan Sosiologi, Universiti Kebangsaan Malaysia, 1976.

Dewan Bahasa dan Pustaka (Malaysia's Language and Literature Agency), *A General Outline of its First Ten-Year Progress and Achievement,* Kuala Lumpur, 1967.

Drummond, Stuart and Hawkins, David, 'The Malaysian Elections of 1969: An Analysis of the Campaign and the Results', *Asian Survey,* Vol. X, No. 4 (April 1970), pp. 320-35.

Economic Development of Malaya, The. Report of a Mission organized by the International Bank for Reconstruction and Development, Government Printer, Singapore, 1955.

Edmonds, I.G., *The New Malaysia,* The Bobbs-Merrill Co. Inc., New York, 1973.

Ee, Joyce, 'Chinese Migration to Singapore, 1896—1941', *Journal of Southeast Asian History,* Vol. 2, No. 1 (March 1961), pp. 33-51.

Emerson, Rupert, *Malaysia, A Study in Direct and Indirect Rule,* University of Malaya Press, Kuala Lumpur, 1966 (reprint).

Endicott, K.M., *An Analysis of Malay Magic,* Clarendon Press, Oxford, 1970.

Enloe, Cynthia H., *Multi-Ethnic Politics: The Case of Malaysia,* University Microfilms, Inc., Ann Arbor, Michigan, 1971.

— 'Issues and Integration in Malaysia', *Pacific Affairs,* Vol. 41:3 (1968).

Esman, Milton Jacob, *Administration and Development in Malaysia; Institution Building and Reform in a Plural Society,* Cornell University Press, Ithaca, 1972.

Fadzil, Sidek, *Sejarah Orang China di Tanah Melayu,* Pustaka Aman Press, Kota Bharu, 1970.

Federation of Malaya and Its Police 1786—1952, The, Government Printer, Kuala Lumpur, 1952.

Fletcher, Nancy McHenry, *The Separation of Singapore from Malaysia,* Cornell University, Ithaca, New York, 1969.

Frank, Wolfgang, 'Chinese into Malaysian', *Far Eastern Economic Review,* 12 March 1965.

Funston, N.J., *Malay Politics in Malaysia, A Study of UMNO and PAS,* Heinemann Educational Books (Asia) Ltd., Kuala Lumpur, 1980.

Gagliano, Felix V., *Communal Violence in Malaysia 1969; the Political Aftermath,* Ohio University Center for International Studies, 1970.

Ghee, Lim Teck and Lowe, Vincent, *Towards A Modern Asia: Aims, Resources and Strategies,* Heinemann Educational Books (Asia) Ltd., Kuala Lumpur, 1976.

Ginsburg, Norton and Roberts, Chester F., Jnr. (eds.), *Malaya,* University of Washington Press, Seattle, 1958.

Goh Cheng Teik, *The May 13th Incident and Democracy in Malaysia,* Oxford University Press, Kuala Lumpur, 1971.

— 'Peking, Kuala Lumpur and the Chinese Minority in Malaysia', *South-East Asian Spectrum,* Vol. 2, No. 2, January 1974, pp. 36-44.

Goldman, Judith, 'Party Support in Western Malaysia: Results of the First Stage of an Ecological Enquiry', *Asian Survey,* June 1971, pp. 582-609.

Green, L.C., 'Indonesia, The United Nations and Malaysia', *Journal of South-east Asian History,* Vol. VI, No. 2 (September 1965), pp. 71-86.

Groves, Henry E., *The Constitution of Malaysia,* Malaysia Publications Ltd., Singapore, 1964.

Gullick, J.M., *Malaysia,* Ernest Benn Ltd., London, 1969.

Hall, D.G.E., *A History of South-East Asia,* Macmillan, London, 1976 (3rd edn.).

Hanrahan, Gene Z., *The Communist Struggle in Malaya,* University of Malaya Press, Kuala Lumpur, 1971.

Heidhues, Mary F. Somers, *Southeast Asia's Chinese Minorities,* Longman Australia Pty. Ltd., 1974.

Henderson, John W., *Area Handbook for Malaysia,* American University, Washington, D.C., 1970.

Hill, R.D., *Rice in Malaya; A Study in Historical Geography,* Oxford University Press, Kuala Lumpur, 1977.

Husin Ali, S., *Malay Peasant Society and Leadership,* Oxford University Press, Kuala Lumpur, 1975.

— *The Malays, Their Problems and Future,* Heinemann Educational Books (Asia) Ltd., Kuala Lumpur, 1981.

Information Malaysia 1975/76, Berita Publishing Sdn. Bhd., Kuala Lumpur, 1975.

Ishak bin Tadin, 'Dato Onn and Malay Nationalism 1946—1951', *Journal of Southeast Asian History,* Vol. I, No. 1 (March 1960), pp. 56-88.

Itagaki, Yoichi, 'Some Aspects of the Japanese Policy for Malaysia under the Occupation, with special reference to Nationalism', in K.G. Tregonning (ed.), *Papers on Malayan History,* University of Malaya in Singapore, 1962, pp. 256-73.

Jackson, R.N., *Immigrant Labour and the Development of Malaya 1786—1920,* Government Press, Kuala Lumpur, 1961.

— *Pickering: Protector of Chinese,* Oxford University Press, Kuala Lumpur, 1965.

Keesing's Contemporary Archives, 1969, pp. 23413-4.

Khoo Kay Kim, *The Western Malay States 1850—1873; The Effects of Commercial Development on Malay Politics,* Oxford University Press, Kuala Lumpur, 1972.

— 'Racial Harmony and Conflict in Southeast Asia: The Example of Malaysia', in *Southeast Asia Today: Problems and Prospects,* Institute of Southeast Asian Studies, Singapore, 1973, pp. 7-15.

Khoo, Gilbert and Lo, Dorothy, *Asian Transformation: A History of South-East, South and East Asia,* Heinemann Educational Books (Asia) Ltd., Singapore, 1977.

Latiff, Subky, 'UMNO: 30 Years After', in *Southeast Asian Affairs 1977,* Institute of Southeast Asian Studies/FEP International Ltd., Singapore, 1977, pp. 160-72.

Lebra, Joyce C., *Japanese-Trained Armies in Southeast Asia,* Heinemann Educational Books (Asia) Ltd., Hong Kong, 1977.

Lee, Alex, 'The Chinese and Malay Dilemmas in Malaysia', *Pacific Community,* No. 3, 1971, pp. 561-71.

Lee, Eddy, *Educational Planning in West Malaysia,* Oxford University Press, Kuala Lumpur, 1972.

Lee Kam Hing (ed.), *The May Tragedy in Malaysia. A Collection of Essays,* Monash University, 1969.

Lee Kuan Yew, *Towards a Malaysian Malaysia,* Government Printing Office, Singapore, 1965.

— *The Battle for a Malaysian Malaysia,* Government Printing Office, Singapore 1965.

Leifer, Michael, 'Singapore in Malaysia: The Politics of Federation', *Journal of Southeast Asian History,* Vol. VI, No. 2 (September 1965), pp. 54-70.

Leigh, Michael B., *The Chinese Community of Sarawak. A Study of Communal Relations,* Malaysia Publishing House Ltd., Singapore, 1964.

Lim, David, *Economic Growth and Development in West Malaysia 1947—1970,* Oxford University Press, Kuala Lumpur, 1973.

Lim Joo Hock, 'Chinese Female Immigration into the Straits Settlements, 1860—1901', *Journal of the South Seas Society,* Vol. XXII, Pts. 1 and 2 (1967), pp. 58-110.

Lim Yoon Lin, 'Malaysia: A Troubled Legacy', in *Southeast Asian Affairs 1977,* Institute of Southeast Asian Studies/FEP International Ltd., Singapore, 1977, pp. 145-59.

Lubis, Mochtar, 'Mysticism in Indonesian Politics', *Solidarity,* Vol. 2, No. 10 (November-December 1967), pp. 22-7.

MacDougall, John Arthur, *Shared Burdens: A Study of Communal Discrimination by the Political Parties of Malaysia and Singapore,* Ann Arbor, Michigan, University Microfilms International, 1978.

Mahathir bin Mohamad, *The Malay Dilemma,* Federal Publications, Singapore, 1977 (3rd reprint).

Malaysia Dalam Tahun 2001 (Malaysia in the Year 2001), Syed Kechik Foundation, Kuala Lumpur, 1975.

Malaysia Year Book, 1970, The Malay Mail, Kuala Lumpur, (n.d.).

Malaysia Year Book, 1973/74, The Malay Mail, Kuala Lumpur, 1974.

Man of Malaysia, A, The New Straits Times Press, Kuala Lumpur, (n.d. 1976?).

Mat Salleh, (pseud. Leon Comber), 'Malays and Chinese Brothers?', *Eastern World,* London, August 1962, p. 20.

Maxwell, Sir George William and Gibson, W.S., *Treaties and Engagements Affecting the Malay States and Borneo,* London, 1924.

May 13 Tragedy, The, A Report, The National Operations Council, Kuala Lumpur, 1969.

Means, Gordon P., 'Special Rights as a Strategy for Development: The Case of Malaysia', *Comparative Politics,* Vol. 5, No. 1 (October 1972), pp. 29-61.

— *Malaysian Politics,* Hodder and Stoughton, London, 1976, (2nd edn.).

Mid-Term Review of the Second Malaysia Plan 1971—75, Government Press, Kuala Lumpur, 1973.

Mills, Lennox, A., *British Malaya, 1824—67,* C.M. Turnbull (ed.), Oxford University Press, Kuala Lumpur, 1966 (reprint).

— *British Rule in Eastern Asia,* The University of Minnesota Press, Minneapolis, 1942.

Milne, R.S., 'National Ideology and Nation-Building in Malaysia', *Asian Survey,* Vol. 10, No. 7, (July 1970), pp. 563-73.

— *Malaya: A Political and Economic Appraisal,* Greenwood Press, Publishers, Westport, Connecticut, 1973 (reprint).

— and Mauzy, Diane K., *Politics and Government in Malaysia,* Federal Publications, Singapore, 1978.

— and Ratnam, K.J., *Malaysia — New States in a New Nation: Political Development of Sarawak and Sabah in Malaysia,* Frank Cass, London, 1974.

Mohamed, Alias, 'The Pan Malayan Islamic Party, A Critical Observation', in *Southeast Asian Affairs 1978,* Institute of Southeast Asian Studies/ Heinemann Educational Books (Asia) Ltd., Singapore, 1978, pp. 165-79.

Morais, Victor J. (ed.), *Strategy for Action, The Selected Speeches of Tun Haji Abdul Razak bin Dato Hussein Al-Haj,* Malaysian Centre for Development Studies, Prime Minister's Department, Kuala Lumpur, 1969.

Mulder, Niels, *Mysticism and Everyday Life in Contemporary Java, Cultural Persistence and Change,* Singapore University Press, 1978.

McIntyre, David, *'Political History 1896—1946'* in Wang Gungwu (ed.), *Malaysia: A Survey,* Pall Mall Press, London, 1964, pp. 138-148.

McTaggart, W.D., *The May 1969 Disturbances in Malaysia: Impact of a Conflict on Developmental Pattern,* Western Conference of the Association for Asian Studies, San Diego, October 1971.

Nam, Tae Yul, *Racism, Nationalism, and Nation-Building in Malaysia and Singapore (A Functional Analysis of Political Integration),* Sadhna Prakashan, Meerut, India, 1973.

— *Malaysia and Singapore: The Failure of a Political Experiment,* University Microfilms International, Ann Arbor, Michigan, 1978.

Ng Siew Yoong, 'The Chinese Protectorate in Singapore', *Journal of Southeast Asian History,* Vol. 2, No. 1 (March 1961), pp. 76-97.

Nyce, Ray (ed.), *Racial Integration as a Process of Development,* Institute for Study of Religions and Society in Singapore and Malaysia, 1972.

Ooi Jin-Bee, *Peninsular Malaysia,* Longman, London, 1976.

O'Ballance, Edgar, *Malaya: The Communist Insurgent War, 1948—1960,* Faber and Faber, Ltd., London, 1966.

Parmer, Norman J., 'Malaysia: Changing A Little to Keep Peace', *Asian Survey,* Vol. 7, No. 2 (February 1967), pp. 131-7.

Png Poh Seng, 'The Kuomintang in Malaya, 1912—1941', *Journal of Southeast Asian History,* Vol. 2, No. 1 (March 1961), pp. 1-32.

Purcell, Victor, *The Chinese in Modern Malaya,* Donald Moore Ltd., Singapore, 1964.

— *The Chinese in Southeast Asia,* Oxford University Press, London, 1965 (2nd edn.).

— *The Chinese in Malaya,* Oxford University Press, London, 1973 (2nd impression).

Puthucheary, James J., *Ownership and Control in the Malayan Economy,* Donald Moore, Singapore, 1960.

Rabushka, Alvin, 'The Manipulation of Ethnic Politics in Malaya', *Polity 2,* No. 3 (Spring 1970) pp. 345-356.

— 'A Note on Overseas Chinese Political Participation in Urban Malaya', *American Political Science Review,* 64, No. 1 (March 1970), pp. 177-8.

— 'Integration in Urban Malaya: Ethnic Attitudes among Malays and Chinese', *Journal of Asian and African Studies 6,* No. 2 (April 1971), pp. 91-107.

— and Shepsle, Kenneth A., *Politics in Plural Societies: A Theory of Democratic Instability,* Charles E. Merrill, Columbus, Ohio, 1972.

— *Race and Politics in Urban Malaya,* Hoover Institute Press, Stanford University, California, 1973.

Rao, Chandriah Appa; Ross-Larson, Bruce; Sopiee, Noordin; and Tjoa Hock Guan, *Issues in Contemporary Malaysia,* Heinemann Educational Books (Asia) Ltd., Kuala Lumpur, 1977.

Ratnam, K.J., *Communalism and the Political Process in Malaya,* University of Malaya Press, Kuala Lumpur, 1967 (reprint).

— 'Constitutional Government and the "Plural Society". Some General Observations', *Journal of Southeast Asian History,* Vol. 2, 1961, pp. 1-10.

— and Milne, R.S., 'The 1969 Parliamentary Election in West Malaysia', *Pacific Affairs,* Vol. XLIII, No. 2, Summer 1970, pp. 203-26.

Rau, Robert L., 'The Development of the Singapore Self-Defence Forces', *Spectrum,* Vol. 3, No. 3, April 1975, pp. 39-43.

Roff, W.R., *The Origins of Malay Nationalism,* University of Malaya Press, Kuala Lumpur, 1967.

Roff, Margaret, 'The Malayan Chinese Association, 1948—65', *Journal of Southeast Asian History,* Vol. VI, No. 2 (September 1965), pp. 40-53.

— 'The Politics of Language in Malaya', *Asian Survey,* Vol. 7, No. 5 (May 1967), pp. 316-328.

Roger, A., *Socialism and Private Enterprise in Equatorial Asia: The Case of Malaysia and Indonesia,* Stanford University, Stanford, California, 1968.

Rudner, Martin, 'The Malaysian General Elections of 1969: A Political Analysis', *Modern Asian Studies,* IV, pt. 1 (January 1970), pp. 1-21.

— *Nationalism, Planning and Economic Modernization in Malaysia: The Politics of Beginning Development,* Sage Publications, Beverley Hills, California, 1975.

Ryan, N.J., *The Making of Modern Malaysia and Singapore,* Oxford University Press, Kuala Lumpur, 1971.

Sadka, Emily, *The Protected Malay States 1874—1875,* University of Malaya Press, Kuala Lumpur, 1971.

Sarasin Viraphol, *The Nanyang Chinese,* Institute of Asian Studies, Faculty of Political Science, Chulalongkorn University, Bangkok, 1972.

Saunders, Graham, *The Development of Plural Society in Malaya,* Longman Malaysia Sdn. Bhd., Kuala Lumpur, 1977.

Second Malaysia Plan 1971—5, Government Press, Kuala Lumpur, 1971.

Shari, Ishak, 'Some Comments on the Eradication of Poverty under the Third Malaysia Plan', in *Southeast Asian Affairs 1977,* Institute of Southeast Asian Studies, Singapore, 1977, pp. 171-81.

Shaw, William, *Tun Razak — His Life and Times,* Longman Malaysia Sdn. Bhd., Kuala Lumpur, 1976.

Short, Anthony, 'Communism, Race and Politics in Malaysia', *Asian Survey,* Vol. 10, No. 12 (December 1970), pp. 1081-9.

— *The Communist Insurrection in Malaya 1948—1960,* Frederick Muller Ltd., London, 1975.

— 'Malaysia: Son of Communist Insurrection', *South-East Asian Spectrum,* Vol. 4, July-September 1976, pp. 1-8.

Silcock, T.H., *The Economy of Malaya,* Eastern Universities Press, Singapore, 1963.

— and Fisk, E.K., *The Political Economy of Independent Malaya,* Australian National University Press, Canberra, 1963.

Simandjuntak, B., *Malayan Federalism, 1945—1963: A Study of Federal Problems in a Plural Society,* Oxford University Press, Kuala Lumpur, 1963.

Simoniya, N.A., *Overseas Chinese in Southeast Asia — A Russian Study,* Data Paper No. 45, Southeast Asia Program, Department of Far Eastern Studies, Cornell University, Ithaca, New York, 1961.

Slimming, John, *Malaysia, Death of a Democracy,* John Murray, London, 1969.

Snider, Nancy L., 'Race, Leitmotiv of the Malaysian Election Drama', *Asian Survey,* X, No. 12, pp. 1070-80.

Soenarno, Rodin, 'Malay Nationalism, 1900—1945', *Journal of Southeast Asian History,* Vol. 1, No. 1 (March 1960), pp. 1-27.

Soh Eng Lim, 'Tan Cheng Lock — His Leadership of the Malayan Chinese', *Journal of Southeast Asian History,* Vol. 1, No. 1, Singapore (March 1960), pp. 34-61.

Sopiee, Mohamed Noordin, *From Malayan Union to Singapore Separation. Political Unification in the Malaysia Region 1945—65,* University of Malaya Press, Kuala Lumpur, 1974.

Stenson, M.R., *Industrial Conflict in Malaya, Prelude to the Communist Revolt of 1948,* Oxford University Press, London, 1970.

Stevenson, Rex, *Cultivators and Administrators, British Educational Policy towards the Malays 1875—1906,* Oxford University Press, Kuala Lumpur, 1975.

Stockwell, A.J., *British Policy and Malay Politics during the Malayan Union Experiment 1942—1948,* Malaysian Branch of the Royal Asiatic Society, Monograph No. 8, Kuala Lumpur, 1979.

Suffian bin Hashim, Mohamed, *An Introduction to the Constitution of Malaysia,* Cetak Kerajaan, Kuala Lumpur, 1972.

Swettenham, Sir Frank, *British Malaya,* George Allen and Unwin Ltd, London, 1948 (3rd edn.).

Tan Cheng Lock, *Malayan Problems: From a Chinese Point of View,* Tannsco, Singapore, 1947.

Tan Ding Eing, *A Portrait of Malaysia and Singapore,* Oxford University Press, Singapore, 1975.

Tarling, Nicholas, *Sukarno and Indonesian Unity,* Heinemann Educational Books, Auckland, 1977.

Tham Seong Chee, *Malays and Modernization,* Singapore University Press, 1977.

Third Malaysia Plan 1976—1980, Government Press, Kuala Lumpur, 1976.

Thompson, Virginia and Adloff, Richard, *Minority Problems in Southeast Asia,* Stanford University Press, Stanford, California, 1955.

Ting Chew Peh, 'Some Problems of Chinese Assimilation in Peninsular Malaysia', in Dahlan, H. (ed.), *The Nescent (sic) Malaysian Society: Development, Trends and Problems,* Jabatan Antropologi dan Sosiologi, Universiti Kebangsaan Malaysia, Kuala Lumpur, 1976, pp. 27-38.

Tjoa Hock Guan, 'Chinese Malaysians and Malaysian Politics', in *Southeast Asian Affairs 1978,* Institute of Southeast Asian Studies/Heinemann Educational Books (Asia) Ltd., Singapore, 1978, pp. 180-90.

Towards National Harmony, Jabatan Cetak Kerajaan, Kuala Lumpur, 1971.

Tregonning, K.G. (ed.), *Papers on Malayan History,* Department of History, University of Malaya in Singapore, 1962.

Turnbull, C.M., *The Straits Settlements, 1826—67: Indian Presidency to Crown Colony,* Oxford University Press, Singapore, 1972.

— 'British Planning for Post-war Malaysia', *Journal of Southeast Asian Studies,* Vol. V, No. 2, September 1974, pp. 239-54.

— *A History of Singapore 1819—1975,* Oxford University Press, Kuala Lumpur, 1977.

Unger, Leonard, 'The Chinese in Southeast Asia', *The Geography Review,* Vol. XXXIV, No. 2 (April 1944), pp. 196-218.

Vasil, R.K., *The Malaysian General Election of 1969,* Oxford University Press, Singapore, 1972.

Von Vorys, K., *Democracy Without Consensus: Communalism and Political Stability in Malaysia,* Princeton University Press, Princeton, 1975.

Wang Gungwu, *A Short History of the Nanyang Chinese,* Eastern Universities Press Ltd., Singapore, 1959.

— 'The Nanhai Trade. A Study of the Early History of Chinese Trade in the South China Sea', *Journal Malayan Branch Royal Asiatic Society,* Vol. XXXI, Pt. 2, No. 182 (June 1958), pp. 1-135.

— (ed.), *Malaysia: A Survey,* Pall Mall Press, London, 1964.

— 'Traditional Leadership in a New Nation: The Chinese in Malaya and Singapore', in Wijayawardene (ed.), *Leadership and Authority: A Symposium,* University of Malaya Press, 1968, pp. 208-22.

— 'Chinese Politics in Malaya', *The China Quarterly,* No. 43 (July-September 1970), pp. 1-30.

— 'Political Change in Malaysia', *Pacific Community,* Vol. 4, No. 4 (1970), pp. 688-90.

Wheeler, L. Richmond, *The Modern Malay,* George Allen and Unwin Ltd., London, 1928.

Who Lives if Malaysia Dies?, Democratic Action Party, Petaling Jaya, Selangor, Malaysia, 1969.

Williams, Lea E., *The Future of the Overseas Chinese in Southeast Asia,* McGraw-Hill Book Co., New York, 1966.

Winstedt, Sir Richard, *The Malay Magician being Shaman, Saiva and Sufi,* Routledge and Kegan Paul, London, 1951.

— *A History of Malaya,* Singapore, 1962.

— *The Malays: A Cultural History,* Kelly and Walsh, Singapore, 1967.

Wong Hoi Kee, Francis, and Ee Tiong Hong, *Education in Malaysia,* Heinemann Educational Books (Asia) Ltd., Hong Kong, 1971.

Yeo Kim Wah, *Political Development in Singapore 1945—55,* Singapore University Press, 1973.

Yong Mun Cheong (ed.), *Trends in Malaysia II, Proceedings and Background Paper,* Singapore University Press for Institute of Southeast Asian Studies, Singapore, 1974.

General Index